Outrageously Fruitful

let go...and let God

MARIA I. MORGAN

OUR GENERATION
PUBLISHING

Published by Our Generation Publishing
© 2015 by
Maria I. Morgan

All rights reserved. No part of this book may be reproduced in any form without permission in writing from the publisher, except in the case of brief quotations embodied in critical articles or reviews.

All Scripture quotations are taken from the Holy Bible, King James Version.

Cover design by Maria I. Morgan

ISBN:9780692474952

Printed in the United States of America

To my wonderful husband, Steve –

This Bible study would not have been possible without your unconditional love, and constant encouragement. This project has taken far longer than I dreamed, and I am truly blessed by your on-going support. Thank you for loving the Lord and for loving me. Over the course of our marriage, you have been a fantastic example of the fruit of the Spirit in action. I love you so much.

Contents

Acknowledgments

I'm so very grateful to each person who has been part of making this Bible study a reality. It has been a team effort. Special thanks to:

Our Generation Publishing team – what an honor to work together to get God's message to the world. Thank you for your confidence and constant encouragement.

Prayer team – your prayers have sustained me through this entire process. Cherie Hill, Patricia Huffman, Darlene King, Sharon LaRocque, Amy Menter, Valeria Seifu, Susan Starnes: thank you for consistently bringing me and this project to the throne of grace. The Lord hears and answers prayer and I'm thankful for each of you. God bless you.

Writers' Critique Group – although we no longer meet together as a group, you have a special place in my heart. Joni Vance, Susan Starnes, Peggy Mueller: your willingness to edit and critique my work each month helped make this a much stronger study. Thank you for investing in me.

Pamela Johnson – your editing comments and suggestions helped tremendously. Thank you for playing a vital role in this project.

Merisa Davis – your class on writing and publishing a Christian book gave me the encouragement I needed to see this project through to completion. Thank you for your passion to see believers publish books of faith.

My Savior – there would be no Bible study without You. Thank You for redeeming me and allowing me to share Your Truth with others. My life is Yours.

Foreword

There is nothing more vital to our faith than studying the Word of God and allowing its truth to permeate our souls on a daily basis. In your efforts to strengthen and perfect your faith, you will find Maria I. Morgan's Bible study, *Outrageously Fruitful*, a blessing beyond all you could hope for or imagine.

Within each devotional you'll find yourself drawing nearer to God and increasing your faith through examination and reflection. It's God's voice you'll hear and His presence you'll experience as you walk in faith through the powerful devotions that will transform your life, page by page.

—Cherie Hill, International Bestselling Christian author

Introduction

Thank you so much for joining me on this adventure! As Christian women, we want to live lives that are fruitful and pleasing to God. The fruit of the Spirit is something we're all familiar with – love, joy, peace, patience, etc., but in a culture that puts self first, what does this fruit look like?

Every day we face situations that are less than ideal. What does our response show a watching world? It's easy to adopt a "what's best for me" mindset. But when we consider God's perspective on the situation, things look much different. Instead of demanding our rights, we're to yield our rights to the control of the Holy Spirit.

It's through this daily yielding that we bring glory to God, and live fruitful lives: "Ye have not chosen me, but I have chosen you, and ordained you, that ye should go and bring forth fruit, and that your fruit should remain…" (John 15:16a)

God's Word is our plumb line. Our Savior wants us to be intimately acquainted with the truth of His Word. It's so important to stay connected to Christ. He is the vine and we are the branches.

As you work through this ten-week study, you'll find five lessons in each chapter. You'll have two extra days each week to catch up if you fall behind. Each character trait of the Spirit is covered in a separate chapter, with a final chapter devoted to review.

The daily lessons are designed to be completed in 15-20 minutes and include four parts: A Moment to Meditate & Memorize; A Life Lesson; A Word from God's Word; and A Time to Reflect. If you're doing this study with a group, you'll find a section at the end of each week, Questions for Group Discussion, to help guide your time together.

The Lord wants to develop a close relationship with you. Let Him speak to you as you begin this journey. Can I pray for you?

Heavenly Father, thank You for loving these ladies more than I can imagine. You make it possible for us to have a relationship with You and to live in a way that brings honor to You and produces fruit that will last through eternity. Help us embrace Your truth and stay connected to You. Give us grace to yield ourselves to Your Holy Spirit. We praise You for what You're doing in our lives. In Jesus' name, Amen.

Now let's choose to abide in Jesus Christ one day at a time and produce a harvest of fruit for Him!

Week 1

Is It Love?

Remember the giddy feeling you experienced the first time you were around that special someone? You may have had butterflies in your stomach or slightly sweaty palms. Was it love? Love is often used in limited terms to describe the heady feelings experienced by couples who have just begun dating. But the Bible defines it as much more than a feeling. This week we'll take a look at the characteristics of love in light of 1 Corinthians 13. We'll identify what it is and recognize what it is not. Let's get started!

This week at a glance:

Day 1 – *Caring Counts*

Day 2 – *Taking the High Road*

Day 3 – *No Place for Pride*

Day 4 – *Green-Eyed Monsters: Not Allowed*

Day 5 – *No Expectations*

Day 1

Caring Counts

A Moment to Meditate & Memorize:

Read the following five verses that describe the characteristics of love. Today, reflect on verse four:

1 Corinthians 13:4-8a *Charity suffereth long, and is kind; charity envieth not; charity vaunteth not itself, is not puffed up. 5 Doth not behave itself unseemly, seeketh not her own, is not easily provoked, thinketh no evil; 6 Rejoiceth not in iniquity, but rejoiceth in the truth; 7 Beareth all things, believeth all things, hopeth all things, endureth all things. 8 Charity never faileth:*

I can imagine love as a multi-faceted gem. It sparkles radiantly when viewed from all different angles. Love has many characteristics. This week we'll discover five of them. In the book of 1 Corinthians, the apostle Paul includes the word "kind" when describing love.

Define "kind" in your own words; then read the definition below: _____

_____

_____

Kind: of a friendly, generous, or warmhearted nature; showing sympathy or understanding, charitable; humane, considerate; forbearing, tolerant; generous, liberal; agreeable, beneficial

A Life Lesson:

Her act of kindness certainly wouldn't make the headlines. Yet her sincere desire to help a friend gave me reason to reflect.

We drove to Florida to see our daughter Riley at college. All week her text messages were charged with excitement. It would be great to see each other. But I knew Riley was also looking forward to the perks of having her parents visit: eating something other than dormitory food, and sleeping at a hotel in a queen-sized bed that was far larger than her twin-sized bunk at the school.

Since we arrived around dinnertime, my husband, daughter, and I decided to get a bite to eat at a nearby restaurant. We settled on Asian cuisine. Talk of egg rolls, sushi, and crab rangoon had our mouths watering. Before we could pull into the restaurant parking lot, however, Riley got a phone call. Her friend Liz was supposed to go visit relatives over the weekend, but her car wouldn't start. She was stuck.

All thoughts of dinner aside, Riley wanted to help. Armed with jumper cables, we headed back to the campus. Hopefully, it would be something that was easy to fix. After several attempts to charge the battery, we realized the problem was more than we could handle. We left Liz and her vehicle in the capable hands of some car repair enthusiasts on campus and headed back to the restaurant.

Fortunately, the campus mechanics were eventually able to diagnose the problem and get Liz's car up and running. But there was one more obstacle. Because of the delay, Liz wouldn't be able to leave until the next day. Her relatives lived several hours away, and she'd have to leave extra early in the morning in order to spend quality time with them. Due to campus policy, she'd be unable to leave early enough to make her trip worthwhile.

Riley to the rescue! Without hesitation, Riley offered Liz the option of staying with us at the hotel so she could get an early start the next morning. Riley had been looking forward to sleeping in the hotel's queen-sized bed with plenty of room to stretch out, yet she was willing to share the bed in order to help a friend. A true act of kindness – caring counts.

Write about an act of kindness that got your attention:_____

_____

_____

A Word from God's Word:

God's Word paints a beautiful picture of the friendship between David and Jonathan. They were kindred spirits. The Bible describes their relationship this way: "And it came to pass, when he had made an end of speaking unto Saul, that the soul of Jonathan was knit with the soul of David, and Jonathan loved him as his own soul," (1 Samuel 18:1).

But all was not peaceful in Jonathan's family. His father was the king of Israel. King Saul had disobeyed the Lord and had been told that his kingdom would be given to someone else. He recognized the hand of God on David's life and began suspecting that the "someone else" was David. He began watching David very closely and plotting his demise.

Needless to say, Jonathan's friendship with David wasn't exactly endorsed by his father. Yet that didn't prevent the two from making an important covenant. Jonathan realized that the kingdom would one day belong to David, and he was willing to give up his right to the throne. He showed immeasurable kindness to David, even standing up to his father in David's defense. Things went from bad to worse with King Saul attempting to kill David. Eventually David had to go into hiding.

David could easily have reacted out of anger toward King Saul and his family, yet David determined to remain true to his part of the covenant.

Read 1 Samuel 20:14-16. Summarize the covenant between Jonathan and David:_____

_____

David demonstrated kindness to Jonathan and his family. David had several opportunities to kill Saul, yet he continued to view Saul as God's anointed king.

Eventually both Jonathan and Saul were killed in battle, and David became king of Israel.

Instead of taking revenge on Saul's household, David kept the covenant he had made with Jonathan years earlier. He began inquiring, "Is there yet any that is left of the house of Saul, that I may show him kindness for Jonathan's sake?" (2 Samuel 9:1).

Read 2 Samuel 9:1-13. To whom did King David show kindness?_____

_____

David treated Mephibosheth as one of his own sons. "And David said unto him, Fear not: for I will surely show thee kindness for Jonathan thy father's sake, and will restore thee all the land of Saul thy father; and thou shalt eat bread at my table continually," (2 Samuel 9:7). What an example! Kindness - a profound characteristic that describes love.

A Time to Reflect:

How does the Lord want you to respond to what He showed you today?_____

_____

_____

Prayer: *Heavenly Father, thank You for Your great kindness toward me. Thank You for life lessons and examples in Your Word that speak to my heart. Help me to walk in the Spirit so I'll be able to practice kindness today. In Jesus' name, Amen.*

Day 2

Taking the High Road

A Moment to Meditate & Memorize:

Focus on verse five:

1 Corinthians 13:4-8a *Charity suffereth long, and is kind; charity envieth not; charity vaunteth not itself, is not puffed up.* **5 Doth not behave itself unseemly, seeketh not her own, is not easily provoked, thinketh no evil;** *6 Rejoiceth not in iniquity, but rejoiceth in the truth; 7 Beareth all things, believeth all things, hopeth all things, endureth all things. 8 Charity never faileth:*

Thoughts are powerful. They influence our decisions and form the groundwork of our plans. Our thoughts become our actions. Puts a whole new perspective on what's going on inside our heads, doesn't it?

In today's lesson we'll take a look at the quality of love that addresses our thinking. Godly love refuses to think evil of others. It reveals a better way. Love takes the high road, and refuses to entertain destructive thoughts about others. According to the apostle Paul love "thinketh no evil," (1 Corinthians 13:5).

Write about a time when you thought negatively about someone based on unconfirmed information:_____

_____

_____

A Life Lesson:

The burly dog appeared from nowhere. His deep growl was menacing. Head lowered, teeth bared, he sped straight toward me and my Golden retriever. His jaws snapped shut on her neck, leaving a trail of blood that discolored her fur. For a minute time stood still. I certainly hadn't anticipated this. We had been minding our own business – enjoying a stroll through the neighborhood – when we'd been caught off guard by this canine attacker. Why had he shot out of his yard totally unprovoked? I was in shock.

Back at home I tried calling the dog's owners. No answer. An e-mail was the next best option. I detailed what had happened – questioning whether their invisible fence was working. And letting them know that their dog's behavior had made me extremely uncomfortable to walk in our neighborhood. I clicked the Send button and settled in to wait for a response.

In the next few hours countless scenarios played through my mind. The owners of the vicious dog were probably just like him. Cold, calculating, mean. I imagined their reply to my e-mail. They probably wouldn't believe that their dog had attacked our retriever. They'd think it was our dog's fault. How dare they think such a thing!

The next morning, as I spent time with my dog, the gash on her swollen neck brought back unpleasant thoughts. Would the neighbors even respond to my e-mail?

Mid-morning I received a phone call. The neighbor couldn't believe her dog had attacked mine. I wasn't surprised. But what she said next caught me off guard. She apologized. She was genuinely concerned that my retriever had been hurt. She and her husband were repairing the break in their invisible fence. By the end of our conversation, my attitude toward the neighbors had changed. They were compassionate, sympathetic people after all!

Thinking evil of others is not a characteristic of love. Love offers the benefit of the doubt.

How can you demonstrate this quality of love today?_____

_____

_____

A Word from God's Word:

Saul was not a very endearing character. In fact, he was the young man who supported the persecution of the early Christians. His name is first mentioned in the book of Acts and is linked to the stoning of Stephen (Acts 7:58). It's clear that Saul wanted to put an end to Christianity and would do anything to achieve this goal: "As for Saul, he made havock of the church, entering into every house, and haling men and women committed them to prison," (Acts. 8:3)

Hot on the trail of the believers, Saul rode furiously toward Damascus. With letter in hand from the high priest, he had gotten permission to take anyone prisoner who professed Jesus Christ (Acts 9:1-2). What began as an ordinary day for Saul, changed into the extraordinary when he came face to face with a blinding light from heaven. He fell to the ground, and heard the voice of God: "...Saul, Saul, why persecutest thou me? And he said, Who art thou, Lord? And the Lord said, I am Jesus whom thou persecutest:" (Acts. 9:4-5a).

Saul was converted and became the apostle Paul – a chosen vessel to share the gospel with Gentiles, kings, and the children of Israel. He was used by God to write much of the New Testament. But Paul's previous reputation was well-known by the disciples. Was this so-called conversion just his ploy to catch them unaware and put them in prison?

Only days after Paul became a believer, the Lord told one of the disciples, Ananias, to go and lay hands on Paul. His sight would be restored and he would be filled with the Holy Ghost. Imagine Ananias' shock and surprise.

What did Ananias say to the Lord? See Acts 9:13-14 _____

_____

_____

Although it would have been easy to respond based on what he knew of Saul, Ananias chose to believe God and act in love – thinking no evil of this persecutor turned believer.

The Christians in Damascus heard him preach in their synagogue: "But all that heard him were amazed, and said; Is not this he that destroyed them which called on this name in Jerusalem, and came hither for that intent, that he might bring them bound unto the chief priests?" (Acts. 9:21).

Then there were the disciples in Jerusalem. When Paul tried to associate with them, they didn't want anything to do with him. The majority of these believers chose to think evil of Paul. But Barnabas was different.

How did Barnabas treat Paul? See Acts 9:27_____

_____

Barnabas did the hard thing, and acted as the go-between. He exemplified love and refused to think evil of Paul. Evaluate how you think of others and choose to put this characteristic into practice today.

A Time to Reflect:

How does the Lord want you to respond to what He showed you?_____

_____

_____

Prayer: Merciful Heavenly Father, thank You for giving me this clear picture of love that doesn't think evil of others. Your Word tells me to love my neighbor as myself and to esteem others highly. Forgive me when my thoughts tear others down. Help me be like Ananias and Barnabas who took the high road and encouraged others. In Jesus' name, Amen.

Day 3

No Place for Pride

A Moment to Meditate & Memorize:

Focus on verse six:

1 Corinthians 13:4-8a *Charity suffereth long, and is kind; charity envieth not; charity vaunteth not itself, is not puffed up.* **5** *Doth not behave itself unseemly, seeketh not her own, is not easily provoked, thinketh no evil;* **6 Rejoiceth not in iniquity, but rejoiceth in the truth;** *7 Beareth all things, believeth all things, hopeth all things, endureth all things. 8 Charity never faileth:*

Have you ever been asked to define a word? Hard, isn't it? It's often easier to describe something in terms of what it is NOT. As we continue to study the characteristics of love, the apostle Paul states that love "is not puffed up," (1 Corinthians 13:4). Simply put, love is not proud.

The Lord is not fond of pride, in fact, it is number one on the list of things He hates (Proverbs 6:17). And oh the problems it causes! "Pride goeth before destruction, and an haughty spirit before a fall," (Proverbs 16:18). Take a look at the dictionary definition of "pride" listed below:

Pride: An excessively high opinion of oneself; conceit. To indulge in self-esteem; glory.

Pride focuses on self, but love shifts the spotlight from self to God. John the Baptist had the right perspective.

Write his words of wisdom from John 3:30 _____

_____

_____

A Life Lesson:

Confession time. Many times I've been tempted to take credit for the gifts and abilities God has given me. Pride begins to swell and I'm convinced I deserve recognition for my accomplishments. I crave the spotlight.

I remember the first time I felt the Holy Spirit's nudge to write. Prior to that time, I had the privilege to participate in and teach Bible studies. But now I was feeling compelled to share what I was learning in written form.

What should I write about? I chose a topic I was familiar with: fund-raising at Pregnancy Care Centers. My goal? To have my article published. It would be difficult but I was up for the challenge. My sister-in-law was a published author and very willing to show me the ropes. Her words of wisdom rang in my ears: "Don't be discouraged if you don't hear from the publisher right away. It usually takes awhile to find the right magazine to publish your article."

Having an idea of what to expect, I got busy. Once the piece was written I typed a query letter, attached my article, and settled down to play the waiting game my sister-in-law had warned me about. But much to my surprise I received an e-mail message just a couple weeks later letting me know that my article had been accepted and would be featured in an up-coming publication.

I was ecstatic. My first attempt at writing an article and not only was it to be published, but I was also being well-paid for my contribution. Pride waltzed onto center stage. My thoughts ran wild – I must be pretty good. Pride began bowing amidst the imagined applause. My mind began to whirl. Another idea for an article tugged at the corner of my mind, and I began calculating the extra money that could be added to our monthly income.

Sure that my second article would be snatched up as quickly as the first, I watched my e-mail daily after it was submitted. Days turned into weeks – nothing. When I finally did hear from the publisher it was to learn that my article didn't have a wide enough appeal for their audience. I couldn't believe it. In a panic I began sending out query letters right and left. I ignored the importance of researching a magazine that would be the perfect fit. Rejection after rejection soon brought discouragement and I stopped writing.

After two full years I met with a writer friend, and once again tuned into the still, small voice of the Holy Spirit. I dusted off my keyboard and got back to writing – but with a different mindset. The purpose of my writing wouldn't be financial gain but would be to make the Lord known. Once again I submitted the article that hadn't been published and this time it was picked up by a Christian women's magazine.

Now when Pride tries to make an appearance there is a spotlight set up in the middle of the stage with its beam cast up to the heavens. It's all about the Lord – it's not about me.

How do you overcome pride in your life?_____

_____

_____

A Word from God's Word:

King Hezekiah. He was known as one of the good kings of Judah. He was an eye-witness of God's protection and provision – yet he battled against pride.

Imagine it. A hostile king from Assyria invaded King Hezekiah's country conquering the cities to the north of Jerusalem. Even as Hezekiah heard the devastating news, the enemy army arrived in his territory, striking fear in the hearts of all. This wasn't just any foe. So far the Assyrians had conquered the cities of Hamath, Arphad, Sepharvaim and Samaria. Jerusalem was next on their list.

The delegates sent by the King of Assyria were pretty intimidating too. Their words were enough to make the bravest warrior among them quake: "...Let not Hezekiah deceive you: for he shall not be able to deliver you. Neither let Hezekiah make you trust in the Lord, saying, The Lord will surely deliver us: this city shall not be delivered into the hand of the king of Assyria. Hearken not to Hezekiah...Beware lest Hezekiah persuade you, saying, The Lord will deliver us. Hath any of the gods of the nations delivered his land out of the hand of the king of Assyria?" (Isaiah 36:14-16a,18). The answer up to this point had been a resounding, "No!"

Instead of giving in to fear King Hezekiah turned to God. Read about it in Isaiah 37:1-8. The Lord provided safety for Hezekiah and his people through a series of unusual events. Not once did Hezekiah and his men have to fight the enemy, making it clear that the hand of God was protecting them.

Check out Isaiah 37:20 and record Hezekiah's reason for wanting deliverance:_____

_____

King Hezekiah wanted to give God the glory.

Years later, the Lord continued to show mercy to Hezekiah when he contracted an illness that threatened his life. Instead of allowing him to die the Lord granted him 15 more years of life. Hezekiah penned words of praise to God for His goodness: "The Lord was ready to save me: therefore we will sing my songs to the stringed instruments all the days of our life in the house of the Lord," (Isaiah 38:20). He was well aware that God provided the cure. To his credit, up to this point we've only observed humility in the life of King Hezekiah. Unfortunately pride made an appearance following his healing.

The king of Babylon and his men heard of Hezekiah's recovery, and showed up on his doorstep with cards and a present. Hezekiah ignored the potential threat posed by the Babylonians, threw open the doors, and took this neighboring king on the royal tour. And what a tour guide he was.

Pride whispered to Hezekiah. He listened too closely and made a big mistake, he "...showed them the house of his precious things, the silver, and the gold, and the spices, and the precious ointment, and all the house of his armour, and all that was found in his treasures: there was nothing in his house, nor in all his dominion, that Hezekiah showed them not," (Isaiah 39:2).

The prophet Isaiah was sent to reprimand Hezekiah for his foolishness. Because he gave in to pride severe repercussions would follow. Read Isaiah 39:6.

What would happen to everything Hezekiah had shown the king of Babylon?

_____

_____

Everything would be taken away. This may seem like a harsh judgment, yet it's important to remember that God HATES pride. Submitting to the Holy Spirit produces a pure love without pride. Seek to honor Him with your choices.

A Time to Reflect:

What has the Lord shown you about pride from today's lesson?_____

_____

_____

Prayer: Loving Heavenly Father, thank You for reminding me that You hate pride. Search me and point out areas where pride has a foothold. Help me submit to Your will so the love of the Holy Spirit will flow through my life, pointing others to You. I love You. In Jesus' name, Amen.

Day 4

Green-Eyed Monsters: Not Allowed

A Moment to Meditate & Memorize:

Today we'll turn our attention to verse 7:

1 Corinthians 13:4-8a *Charity suffereth long, and is kind; charity envieth not; charity vaunteth not itself, is not puffed up. 5 Doth not behave itself unseemly, seeketh not her own, is not easily provoked, thinketh no evil; 6 Rejoiceth not in iniquity, but rejoiceth in the truth;* **7 Beareth all things, believeth all things, hopeth all things, endureth all things.** *8 Charity never faileth:*

Do you ever compare yourself with others? I do – even though I know it's not wise (2 Corinthians 10:12). When I notice a quality in someone else that I'm lacking, feelings of envy often get the best of me. I become a green-eyed monster who desires to have the positive attribute of the other person. But envy is NOT one of the characteristics of love. Paul puts it this way in the famous love chapter: "Charity (love) suffereth long, and is kind; charity envieth not..." (1 Corinthians 13:4a).

In your own words, define "envy":_____

_____

Envy: a feeling of discontent and resentment aroused by another's desirable possessions or qualities, accompanied by a strong desire to have them for oneself

A Life Lesson:

Her charisma is immediately evident. She has a way with words that indicates a rare gift. And she has a heart of compassion that demonstrates her concern for others. How can I possibly measure up?

When I think about her qualities a part of me wants to scream, "It's not fair!" Slowly the green-eyed monster of Envy is jostled awake. Why can't I attract others like she does? I'm not shy by any means, and I really DO care about others. So why does she seem to get center stage while I am relegated to the shadows? I fuss and fume wrestling with my discontent. Envy is now wide awake.

As Envy reaches a gnarled hand toward the keys dangling outside her cell, a glimmer of truth pierces my mind. A simple Bible verse memorized years ago captures my thoughts: "I will praise thee; for I am fearfully and wonderfully made: marvellous are thy works; and that my soul knoweth right well, " (Psalm 139:14). True, I may not possess the qualities of my friend, but I am made in the image of God, right? Isn't that a good reason to rejoice and give Him praise?

Envy isn't about to give up the fight, and she continues to finger the keys that will set her free. Thoughts of rejoicing and praise degenerate into "if only" thinking. If only I had been equipped with my friend's abilities I could accomplish so much more. I'd be so much happier wouldn't I? Envy now has the keys in her hand, fumbling with them in an attempt to find the one that will unlock her cell door.

As good and evil fight for dominance within me, a friend's strategically sent e-mail points me back to the truth of God's Word. As I ponder the fact that God creates each of us with unique gifts and abilities, I realize that He equipped me with exactly what I need to bring Him ultimate glory.

I am convinced of this truth, and Envy knows she has been beaten. The keys she holds in her hand clatter to the ground and she falls to the floor in a heap.

When I keep my thoughts focused on pleasing my Master by using the abilities He's given me, I avoid the mistake of comparing myself with others. I'm able to praise God for the way He created me AND point others to Him.

Do you recall a time when you were envious? How did you handle it?_____

_____

_____

A Word from God's Word:

Saul was the first king of the nation of Israel. An impressive warrior, he made quite a name for himself on the battlefield. Why should this battle be any different? The Israelites were pitted against their arch-enemies, the Philistines. The Philistines sent out their warrior Goliath to challenge Saul and his army. Imagine the scene: the giant Goliath, in full battle gear, demanding that Saul and his army choose a man to fight with him.

The stakes were high. The army of the defeated warrior would become the winning armies' slaves. Saul had a choice to make: respond in faith or in fear. Look at his response: "When Saul and all Israel heard those words of the Philistine, they were dismayed, and greatly afraid," (1 Samuel 17:11).

Describe how the attitude of a leader can affect those who follow him/her:___

_____

_____

_____

David arrived on the scene, with food for his brothers. He was just in time to witness Goliath's diatribe. David was outraged at the giant's audacity and volunteered to fight him. He was just a young shepherd boy with a big faith in his God. David rehearsed God's faithfulness in the ears of King Saul: "The Lord that delivered me out of the paw of the lion, and out of the paw of the bear, he will deliver me out of the hand of this Philistine," (1 Samuel 17:37).

God allowed David to kill Goliath using nothing more than a slingshot and a smooth stone. The Israelites were ecstatic! "And it came to pass as they came, when David was returned from the slaughter of the Philistine, that the women came out of all cities of Israel, singing and dancing, to meet king Saul, with tabrets, with joy and with instruments of musick. And the women answered one another as they played, and said, Saul hath slain his thousands, and David his ten thousands," (1 Samuel 18:6-7).

Read 1 Samuel 18:8-9. How did King Saul respond to this song?_____

_____

_____

The women's song didn't sit well with King Saul – thousands were attributed to him, but ten times as many were attributed to David. A seed of envy was planted in Saul's heart. Left unchecked, the seed would sprout and begin to grow. Saul allowed his imagination to run wild and it wasn't long before he was planning to kill David. Saul twisted an innocent song of thanksgiving into a death sentence for the young man he viewed as his rival.

King Saul was consumed with envy, and on numerous occasions he attempted to impale David to the palace wall with his spear. Eventually David had to run for his life. But instead of quenching Saul's envy David's departure added fuel to the fire. Saul and his army relentlessly pursued David for many years.

Saul's example was a sad case of envy out of control. Had he refused to give in to his envy, his story may have turned out differently.

Envy. A powerful vice that can destroy a life. Follow after the love produced by the Spirit and envy won't find a foothold.

A Time to Reflect:

How does the Lord want you to respond to what He showed you about envy?

_____

_____

_____

Prayer: *Gracious Heavenly Father, thank You for teaching me about the characteristics of love. I know envy is not one of them. Help me identify it and purge it from my heart. Thank You for the way of escape You provide when I'm tempted to be envious of others. In Jesus' name, Amen.*

Day 5

No Expectations

A Moment to Meditate & Memorize:

Let's consider verse 8:

1 Corinthians 13:4-8a *Charity suffereth long, and is kind; charity envieth not; charity vaunteth not itself, is not puffed up. 5 Doth not behave itself unseemly, seeketh not her own, is not easily provoked, thinketh no evil; 6 Rejoiceth not in iniquity, but rejoiceth in the truth; 7 Beareth all things, believeth all things, hopeth all things, endureth all things.* **8 Charity never faileth:**

You spend hours cooking a gourmet meal. Each dish is a masterpiece. As your family sits down to dinner, conversation revolves around work and school. Although you didn't expect the meal to be the main topic discussed, you DID think someone would make mention of the delicious food. But nothing is said. How do you respond?

Would you be a bit offended? A pout might replace the smile on your face. But how would love react? True love gives – it gives without expecting anything in return. The apostle Paul doesn't mince words: "Charity (love)...seeketh not her own..." (1 Corinthians 13:5). That's a tall order - impossible without the power of an Almighty God.

Do you remember a time when you demonstrated this characteristic of love? Describe it:_____

_____

_____

A Life Lesson:

My husband. I'm so thankful for him. The Lord knew exactly what I needed in a marriage partner, and boy, did He deliver. Steve is a godly man, has an even temperament, provides for our family, and loves unselfishly. He's willing to sacrifice his own comfort in order to make us comfortable.

Countless examples of his kindness are etched in my memory. I remember when I was pregnant with our daughter. Steve offered to give me a backrub following an especially long day at work. Tense muscles relaxed and I felt human again. Over twenty years later, my man seldom ends a day without giving me a backrub! Yes, I know I'm spoiled!

There were the tension-filled days after our baby girl was born. As new parents, we weren't quite sure what to do with this little life that had been entrusted to us. No manual accompanied our tiny bundle. Colic further complicated things. Her crying added to our feelings of helplessness.

Nothing seemed to console her. Steve knew I was frustrated. He'd return from a challenging day at the office, scoop Riley into his arms, and encourage me to take a break for awhile. Truth be told, he needed a break too but was willing to deny himself the luxury.

Fast forward to the present. Little things he does make a big difference. There are times when I absent-mindedly misplace something, and Steve is right there. Willing to set aside what he's doing and join in the search. Then there are the times he encourages me to stretch out on the couch while he sits on the other end with my feet in his lap. And more often than not, he's even agreeable to switching TV stations from the History channel to HGTV. What a man!

I continue to learn a lot from this wonderful man I married. His example of selfless love stands out in my mind, challenging me to put others first. Challenging me to give of myself, expecting nothing in return.

How will you show this type of love today?_____

_____

_____

A Word from God's Word:

The Lord Jesus Christ. Could there be a more perfect example of love that "...seeketh not her own?" From the very foundations of the world God loved us. He formed man out of the dust of the ground with his own two hands, and "breathed into his nostrils the breath of life; and man became a living soul," (Genesis 2:7).

Man's perfect fellowship with his Creator didn't last long. Adam and Eve sinned. And sin had a hefty price tag. But God had a plan. It involved a sacrifice – the sacrifice of His only Son, Jesus Christ. Jesus was willing to lay aside His glory, humble Himself, and take on the form of a man, in order to fulfill His Father's plan.

In God's perfect timing, He sent His Son to be born of a virgin. Fully God yet fully man. He grew up much like other boys in His town but He never fell to temptation. He lived a sinless life. The law of the Old Testament was satisfied – making Him the only one able to pay the sin debt for mankind.

Even in our sin-ridden state, God loved us. His selfless love is echoed throughout the pages of scripture. "For when we were yet without strength, in due time Christ died for the ungodly...But God commendeth his love toward us, in that, while we were yet sinners, Christ died for us," (Romans 5:6,8). And again in John 3:16.

Write the familiar passage in the space provided:_____

_____

_____

_____

Jesus gave His life in order to restore our relationship with a holy God. He doesn't require us to DO anything to earn this restored fellowship. In fact, it can't be earned because it is a gift. The only decision we have to make is whether or not to receive His gift. Not everyone wants the free gift. Take a look at the response of some of the people in Jesus' day: "He was in the world, and the world was made by him, and the world knew him not. He came unto his own, and his own received him not," (John 1:10-11).

This attitude was not unusual while Jesus walked the earth. However, He didn't let it keep him from completing His mission. He had a single focus: "For I came down from heaven, not to do mine own will, but the will of him that sent me," (John 6:38). And that focus led Him to Calvary. Even as He hung on the cross, He continued to exemplify love.

What was Jesus' prayer to His Father in Luke 23:34?_____

_____

_____

His words were spoken for the mockers who denied His deity, "...Father, forgive them; for they know not what they do..." (Luke 23:34).

He continues to extend His selfless love today: "The Lord is not slack concerning his promise, as some men count slackness; but is longsuffering to us-ward, not willing that any should perish, but that all should come to repentance," (2 Peter 3:9). Do you realize that your sin has plunged you into debt? A debt that you can never repay?

The good news is Jesus loves you. He loves you so much, that He died on the cross to pay your sin debt. Have you accepted His gift?

A Time to Reflect:

How does the Lord want you to respond to the lesson today?_____

_____

_____

Prayer: *Gracious Heavenly Father, thank You for Your selfless love. Before there was time, You knew me and loved me, and had a plan for bringing me back into fellowship with You. Thank You for the free gift of salvation that cost Your Son His life. Help me submit to Your Spirit so I can demonstrate this characteristic of love to those who don't know You. In Jesus' name, Amen.*

Questions for Group Discussion:

1. List the five characteristics of love that were outlined this week. Give an example of each.

2. How do your thoughts affect your treatment of others? (Read Acts 9:13-17, 21, 27 for examples)

3. Pride is not a characteristic of love. When pride has a foothold, where is your focus? What should you be focused on?

4. Love and lust are often confused in our society. What is the difference?

5. Which characteristic of love discussed this week, is most difficult for you to demonstrate? Spend some time in prayer humbly yielding yourself to the Lord in this area.

Jesus, Others, You: The Right Way to Spell Joy

Happiness and joy are two words that are often used interchangeably. But there IS a difference. While happiness is experienced when circumstances or events are going well, joy is an attitude of the heart that remains constant no matter what. This week we'll explore how a vibrant relationship with Christ establishes lasting joy. With the proper priorities – Jesus, others, and you, a pathway is paved for a life filled with this fruit of the Spirit – joy.

This week at a glance:

Day 1 – *An Attitude of the Heart*

Day 2 – *Spelling it Right*

Day 3 – *Joy in the Journey*

Day 4 – *Eyes on the Prize*

Day 5 – *Reason to Rejoice*

Day 1

An Attitude of the Heart

A Moment to Meditate & Memorize:

This week we'll discover some of the characteristics of joy. Read and study our verse:

Romans 15:13 *Now the God of hope fill you with all joy and peace in believing, that ye may abound in hope, through the power of the Holy Ghost.*

We're happy when things are going our way – we have money to cover the bills, our kids are behaving, and that long-awaited vacation is only a week away. But what happens when circumstances don't line up? Or when they skid out of control?

There's a big difference between happiness and joy. Happiness is subject to circumstances. Joy is an attitude of the heart. Today we'll discuss the key to this important fruit of the Spirit.

A Life Lesson:

Our wedding. Although it took place many years ago, I still remember the excitement of that day and the thrill of beginning a new life with the man I loved. From the primping and pictures, to the walk down the aisle and the "I do's," the day was nothing short of a joyous celebration.

I didn't know what the future would hold, but I knew my husband Steve was the man God intended for me. It was a source of great joy to know that Steve and I were on the same page spiritually. We both agreed to keep the Lord first in our lives as we navigated through our marriage. We didn't think things would be perfect, yet we knew with God at the center of our relationship, our marriage would be strong. A source of great hope.

Marriage was instituted by God himself. Moses wrote about it in the book of Genesis: "And the Lord God said, It is not good that the man should be alone; I will make him an help meet for him...And the Lord God caused a deep sleep to fall upon Adam, and he slept: and he took one of his ribs, and closed up the flesh instead thereof; And the rib, which the Lord God had taken from man, made he a woman, and brought her unto the man. And Adam said, This is now bone of my bones, and flesh of my flesh: she shall be called Woman, because she was taken out of Man. Therefore shall a man leave his father and his mother, and shall cleave unto his wife: and they shall be one flesh," (Genesis 2: 18,21-24).

Marriage was designed by God to bring joy. And I've been blessed to experience much happiness throughout our years of marriage as well: the birth of our daughter, job promotions, and fun family vacations. But even during the tough times: when I experienced miscarriages, our daughter got sick, or my husband lost his job, I was able to remain joyful – knowing that I could trust the Lord with the circumstances in my life.

I agree whole-heartedly with the Psalmist, David. Having faith in the Lord Jesus brings joy. "But let all those that put their trust in thee rejoice: let them ever shout for joy, because thou defendest them: let them also that love thy name be joyful in thee," (Psalm 5:11). His Word is true, and He never changes. He is the source of true joy.

Describe a time when things weren't going well, yet you experienced joy in spite of the circumstances: _____

_____

A Word from God's Word:

I have to admit that the story of Esther is one of my all-time favorites. The way the Lord was able to use a young woman to save the Jewish people is nothing short of miraculous. Orphaned as a child and raised by her cousin Mordecai, Esther had no idea that one day she would become the queen of Persia.

One of many beautiful young ladies, Esther was taken from her home to participate in a beauty pageant. King Ahasuerus was choosing a new queen. An elaborate beauty treatment was completed before each young woman was brought before the king. With so much competition, what was the likelihood that Esther would be chosen? But God had a plan.

With whom did the Lord allow Esther to find favor? (Esther 2:8-9)_____

_____

The Bible records King Ahasuerus' response to Esther: "And the king loved Esther above all the women, and she obtained grace and favour in his sight more than all the virgins; so that he set the royal crown upon her head, and made her queen instead of Vashti," (Esther 2:17). I can only imagine how Esther must have felt – excited, yet nervous about all the responsibilities that came with being queen.

It didn't take long for the giddiness to wear off. There was trouble in the kingdom. Someone wanted to kill the Jews. And it was none other than the head of Ahasuerus' princes: Haman. But what could Esther do about it? When letters arrived throughout the land, confirming that the Jews were indeed to be killed on the thirteenth day of the month Adar, Mordecai sent a message to Esther.

What was Mordecai's advice to Esther? (Esther 4:8)_____

_____

Didn't Mordecai understand? It wasn't that easy. If she went before the king without being summoned, and Ahasuerus didn't hold out the golden scepter to her, she would be put to death. But Mordecai's response made her reconsider: "Think not with thyself that thou shalt escape in the king's house, more than all the Jews. For if thou altogether holdest thy peace at this time, then shall there enlargement and deliverance arise to the Jews from another place; but thou and thy father's house shall be destroyed: and who knoweth whether thou art come to the kingdom for such a time as this?" (Esther 4:13-14).

After much fasting and prayer, Esther approached the king. Imagine her relief when Ahasuerus extended the golden scepter and agreed to attend the banquet she had proposed. The banquet offered her the perfect opportunity to uncover Haman's wicked plot to destroy her and her people. Although the law that had originally been decreed could not be revoked, Ahasuerus gave Esther and

Mordecai permission to write a new law that allowed the Jews to defend themselves against the upcoming attacks that were planned.

Picture the Jews response. As the letters were delivered, joyous celebration broke out. Although their enemies may still try to harm them, they were overjoyed that they could now defend themselves. Now there was a glimmer of hope where only days before there had been hopelessness.

Before any victories were won, the people were filled with joy: "The Jews had light, and gladness, and joy, and honour. And in every province, and in every city, whithersoever the king's commandment and his decree came, the Jews had joy and gladness, a feast and a good day. And many of the people of the land became Jews; for the fear of the Jews fell upon them," (Esther 8:16-17).

Joy. A powerful fruit of the Spirit that was present in spite of difficult circumstances. A fruit that yielded hope. Find your joy in the Lord.

A Time to Reflect:

Are you able to be joyful in spite of challenging circumstances? How does the Lord want you to respond today?_____

_____

_____

Prayer: Heavenly Father, thank You for showing me that I can choose to be joyful in spite of my circumstances. This life is about serving You and pointing others to You. Help me to exercise joy today. In Jesus' name, Amen.

Day 2

Spelling it Right!

A Moment for Meditation & Memorization:

Begin memorizing this week's verse.

Romans 15:13 *Now the God of hope fill you with all joy and peace in believing, that ye may abound in hope, through the power of the Holy Ghost.*

It's easiest to experience joy when I spell it right. No, I'm not talking about the letters – j, o, and y. But putting those letters in the right order gives me the perspective I need: Jesus, others, and you. When I approach life by giving Jesus first place, then concentrate on the needs of others, God provides for my needs and the fruit of joy follows.

Take a few moments to pray before continuing.

A Life Lesson:

Remember mastering the art of spelling in grade school? Today we're exploring the simple word: joy. Oddly enough, it can be these short, seemingly easy words that give us the most trouble.

Writing can be a very isolating job. It's not unusual for a day to go by with very little interaction with others. Don't get me wrong – I love what I do. And technology makes it possible for me to communicate with others via my keyboard. But if I don't purposely schedule face to face time with people, I can become task-oriented and retreat into my own little world.

The more I have to accomplish, the easier it is for me to misspell "j-o-y." I get it all mixed up and end up with weird combinations like: "y-j-o," "y-o-j," or sometimes it's "y-y-y." Sadly, those are the days I think life is all about me.

37

No doubt your days are different than mine. But I have a sneaking suspicion we all struggle with the same thing. Consider the following scenario – you wake up a bit late and have to skip your time of fellowship with the Lord in order to make it to work. The phone calls and meetings are non-stop through the lunch hour. On your way home, you avoid calls from friends and family because you need time to unwind. You finish the day cooped up in your office completing work your boss needed yesterday.

As you head down the hall to tuck your kids into bed, you realize the house is quiet. The lights have been turned out. Everyone is in bed, and you missed spending time with your family because you had too many things to accomplish.

Sometimes it's unavoidable. The bottom line? It's important to submit our agenda to the Lord, so He can schedule the divine interruptions we so desperately need. I'm not sure how He does it, but oftentimes His interruptions will allow us to accomplish so much more.

Time spent with the Lord in Bible study helps us get the letter "j" in the right place. Jesus comes first. Prayer reminds us of the needs of others. So far, the letters are lining up in the right order: "j-o." Throughout the day, as we're aware of the Holy Spirit's promptings, we're able to offer a word of encouragement to our spouse, share the gospel with the grocer, lend a sympathetic ear to the neighbor, correct our child in love, and still accomplish the work that's required of us.

With all the letters in the proper order, the result is beautiful: joy!

A Word from God's Word:

Who could have guessed that a widow would play a significant role in the life of the prophet, Elijah? The Old Testament records the story of this woman who knew how to spell "joy." Although she remains nameless, her example is worth emulating.

King Ahab had led the children of Israel into sin. Worship of the false god, Baal was rampant. The Lord was very displeased. He sent the prophet Elijah to speak to the king. A severe drought would plague the land because of Ahab's rebellion. Without rain what would happen to the crops and streams?

The Lord led Elijah to the brook Cherith where He miraculously provided for him.

According to 1 Kings 17:6, what did Elijah eat and drink?_____

_____

Having bread and meat delivered morning and evening by ravens had to be incredible. But when the brook dried up, the Lord had further instructions for Elijah: "Arise, get thee to Zarephath, which belongeth to Zion, and dwell there: behold, I have commanded a widow woman there to sustain thee," (1 Kings 17:9). First the Lord had used birds that were considered unclean to provide for Elijah, and now He was going to use a widow who was a foreigner to sustain him. How very unusual.

When he got to the city gate, he saw a woman gathering sticks. Weary from his long journey he asked her for a drink. As she turned away to get him some water, he made one further request: "Bring me, I pray thee, a morsel of bread in thine hand," (1 Kings 17:11b).

How did she respond to his request (1 Kings 17:12)?_____

_____

_____

She was truthful – she didn't have much: just a handful of meal and a little oil. Yet Elijah's words confirmed what she had been told by the Lord. Elijah encouraged her to make him some food first, and then make food for herself and her son. He reassured her with a promise from the Lord: "The barrel of meal shall not waste, neither shall the cruse of oil fail, until the day that the Lord sendeth rain upon the earth," (1 Kings 17:14).

The Lord had told her to sustain this prophet (1 Kings 17:9). She obeyed. By putting the Lord first, and the needs of others second, this precious widow's needs were also met.

Did the Lord keep His promise to the widow (1 Kings 17:16)?_____

A Time to Reflect:

How have you been spelling "joy"? How does the Lord want you to respond today?_____

_____

_____

Prayer: Heavenly Father, thank You for reminding me of the right way to spell "joy." Help me to put You first, and others second, knowing that when I do, You'll take care of me too. Forgive me when I put myself first. I love You Lord, and am thankful for the joy You give me. In Jesus' name, Amen.

Day 3

Joy in the Journey

A Moment to Meditate & Memorize:

Continue memorizing our verse.

Romans 15:13 *Now the God of hope fill you with all joy and peace in believing, that ye may abound in hope, through the power of the Holy Ghost.*

Life is a journey filled with surprises. Some good. Others not as good. I know when I reach heaven one day I will be completely satisfied and content to be in the presence of my Savior. But until that day, I can still experience joy in my journey here on earth.

After Jesus' resurrection, He sent the Holy Spirit to indwell all believers and help them in a very special way: " But the Comforter, which is the Holy Ghost, whom the Father will send in my name, he shall teach you all things, and bring all things to your remembrance, whatsoever I have said unto you," (John 14:26).

As you and I submit to the Holy Spirit, He enables us to understand God's Word, and gives us the strength and ability to complete the work the Lord has for us (Ephesians 2:10). Being a part of the Master's plan brings great joy. And the guarantee of a home in heaven increases that joy exponentially!

A Life Lesson:

I enjoy container gardening. It's always fun to decide what I'll plant in each pot. Some nutrient-rich soil, water and sunshine, and my plants are off to a good start.

This year, I decided to try tomato plants. There's nothing better than a red, ripe, juicy tomato to add flavor to any meal. Although my plants were small, I was convinced they would yield a nice harvest. That was before the torrential downpour.

As I stood on the deck assessing the damage to my plants, I realized one of them had been snapped in half. The top of the plant was still leafy and green, but I knew it wouldn't be able to produce any tomatoes since it was no longer attached to the stem. It would soon wither because it couldn't receive any nutrients. There was a lesson here.

Just like the entire tomato plant needs to be connected to the stem in order to grow and produce physical fruit, I need to be attached to Christ in order to produce spiritual fruit. Jesus paints a powerful word picture: "I am the true vine, and my Father is the husbandman…Abide in me, and I in you. As the branch cannot bear fruit of itself, except it abide in the vine; no more can ye, except ye abide in me," (John 15:1,4).

Abiding in Christ is the key. The Father is doing the work of the husbandman – weeding, pruning, fertilizing. He gives me everything I need to be fruitful. As I abide in Christ, and allow the Father to clean me up, fruit will be produced. When I bear fruit the Father is glorified (John 15:8).

Spectacular news! I'm not required to keep a list of rules or strive to prove my love for Christ – instead, I'm invited to abide in Christ and allow the Father to work in my life. He works patiently to eliminate the things that hinder my growth and I am able to produce fruit that pleases Him.

The added bonus? Not only is glory given to the Father, but I receive something as well – joy. Now that's a great deal.

Write John 15:11 in the space provided:_____

_____

_____

A Word from God's Word:

The early believers didn't have the same freedom to worship as we have today. The Jewish believers were discouraged. Opposition increased daily toward those who claimed Jesus Christ as Savior. Throughout the world, it seemed like those in charge were trying frantically to stamp out all followers of the Way.

King Herod himself, willing to appease the Jewish leaders, had killed the apostle James. What would happen next? I can imagine the believers gathering secretly for fear of persecution. It may have happened like this. . .

As they met together in secret at Matthias' house, the believers heard sudden footsteps outside. A knock on the door followed. Silence descended on the group as the believers exchanged terrified glances. Their anxiety quickly turned to relief when Aristarchus entered.

Aristarchus had received a cleverly concealed letter from one of the other groups of believers – and it had been written by the apostle Peter himself! What had begun as a discouraging day suddenly seemed much brighter. A hush fell over the

42

group as Aristarchus reached into his bag and carefully removed the weathered scroll.

How encouraging to be reminded of God's great mercy and the inheritance that awaited each of them in heaven. His words served as a balm, lifting their spirits in spite of the persecution they faced.

As he read the final sentences, Aristarchus' voice grew stronger. "That the trial of your faith, being much more precious than of gold that perisheth, though it be tried with fire, might be found unto praise and honour and glory at the appearing of Jesus Christ: Whom having not seen, ye love; in whom, though now ye see him not, yet believing, ye rejoice with joy unspeakable and full of glory," (1 Peter 1:7-8).

The believers savored each word as if it were a delicious feast. What seemed impossible only hours before, was no longer so. They could live encouraged, joyful lives. Faith replaced fear. Faith in a Savior who gave His life for each one of them, was worth dying for.

They realized their mission was to live for Christ, making Him known in the corner of the world where they lived. And although persecution was guaranteed, Peter's words reminded them that the trial of their faith would produce praise, honor, and glory for the Lord. Even death could only serve to usher in each believer's incorruptible inheritance – an eternity spent with Jesus Christ!

As Aristarchus carefully rolled up the scroll, the believers expressed their renewed joy in prayer and worship.

Write a prayer to the Lord expressing your joy for what He's doing in your life:_____

_____

_____

_____

A Time to Reflect:

Are you abiding in Christ? How does the Lord want you to respond today?__

_____

_____

Prayer: *Heavenly Father, thank You for the lessons from the early church. Forgive me when I quench the work of the Holy Spirit. Help me abide in Christ, and submit to Your pruning process. Help me keep my eyes fixed on You, remembering that my eternal home is in heaven. Thank You for letting me experience joy. In Jesus' name, Amen.*

Day 4

Eyes on the Prize

A Moment to Meditate & Memorize:

Continue memorizing this week's verse.

Romans 15:13 *Now the God of hope fill you with all joy and peace in believing, that ye may abound in hope, through the power of the Holy Ghost.*

Maintaining a joyful attitude in spite of opposition is difficult. Whether the opponent is a person or a thing, it's easy to focus on the problem and get discouraged from the task at hand.

But we have the ultimate role model: Jesus Christ. He faced the most difficult challenge – dying for the sins of all mankind. What did he focus on? "Looking unto Jesus the author and finisher of our faith; who for the joy that was set before him endured the cross, despising the shame, and is set down at the right hand of the throne of God," (Hebrews 12:2).

He focused on the joy of knowing His redeeming work would make it possible for us to spend an eternity with Him.

A Life Lesson:

Sometimes they're easy. But many times they take much longer than I anticipate. Projects. Everyone has them. Whether it's just organizing a linen closet, or gearing up to repaint the interior of the house, each project takes careful planning and follow through.

One project we battle constantly is keeping our creek and pond flowing normally. Every time we experience a heavy rain, debris washes into our creek from upstream forming a dam that blocks the water flow into our pond. The result? A full day of work cleaning up what the rain left behind.

The most recent cleanup project came on the heels of a particularly heavy downpour. As I stared at the massive mess clogging our creek, I wasn't exactly joyful. In fact, truth be told I was a bit angry – angry with the neighbors upstream who had stacked their yard debris too close to the creek. Now I would have to clean it up.

As I piled branches and leaf debris on the bank of the creek, I couldn't deny the truth that pushed its way to the forefront of my mind. My life often resembles the clogged creek. Sometimes life's problems and concerns overwhelm me, leaving a mess in their wake. How grateful I am that the Lord patiently cleans up my messes as I confess them and surrender them to Him.

Things like:

*pride

*anxiety

*a critical spirit

He faithfully points out these weaknesses, all the while offering His strength to overcome them. Definitely something to be joyful about!

By the time I was done cleaning up all the debris, the creek was once again flowing, and I could say with the Psalmist David: "Restore unto me the joy of thy salvation; and uphold me with thy free spirit," (Psalm 51:12).

Describe a time when a renewed relationship with the Lord brought you joy:

_____

_____

_____

A Word from God's Word:

It was hard to believe. After 70 years in exile, the people from Judah were finally allowed to return to their homeland. They knew a major project loomed before them – they would have to rebuild their city.

The first structure they would rebuild was the Temple. Following 70 long years in captivity, the people knew the importance of putting God first. They spent much time carefully planning the layout of this house. And when the foundation was laid, songs of praise and thanksgiving were offered to the Lord.

But when something was done for the Lord, opposition soon followed. And the children of the captivity didn't have to wait long: "Then the people of the land weakened the hands of the people of Judah, and troubled them in building, And hired counselors against them, to frustrate their purpose, all the days of Cyrus king of Persian, even until the reign of Darius king of Persia," (Ezra 4:4-5). The plan of those who opposed the work of God was successful.

What happened according to Ezra 4:24? _____

_____

Fear overcame the joy of those who were building, and they stopped the work until the second year Darius was king of Persia. But encouragement was waiting in the wings in the form of two prophets, Haggai and Zechariah. Two motivated men, Zerubbabel and Jeshua, resumed construction on the Temple after hearing the prophets speak.

The arrows of opposition continued to fly, but Zerubbabel and Jeshua were not going to be deterred. It took a letter from King Darius to put the opponents in their place: "Let the work of this house of God alone; let the governor of the Jews and the elders of the Jews build this house of God in his place," (Ezra 6:7). It was a miracle.

And if that wasn't enough to restore the people's joy, what else did King Darius decree (Ezra 6:8-9, 11)?_____

_____

_____

When God provided, He did so in a way that left no questions. His work went forward and was completed. The people's response? "And the children of Israel, the priests, and the Levites, and the rest of the children of the captivity, kept the dedication of this house of God with joy," (Ezra 6:16).

Trusting the Lord in spite of opposition isn't easy. But take joy in the work He has for you knowing that it will be accomplished.

A Time to Reflect:

Do you tend to lose your joy when you face opposition to the work God has given you? How does the Lord want you to respond today?_____

_____

_____

Prayer: *Heavenly Father, thank You for letting me be involved in Your work. I know I will face opposition just like the children of Israel did. Help me to maintain an attitude of joy and to trust You to continue working even when it gets difficult. In Jesus' name, Amen.*

Day 5

Reason to Rejoice

A Moment to Meditate & Memorize:

Finish memorizing this week's verse.

Romans 15:13 *Now the God of hope fill you with all joy and peace in believing, that ye may abound in hope, through the power of the Holy Ghost.*

Joy and rejoicing often go hand in hand. When I'm filled with joy, it's natural for me to express it verbally. It was no different when the angels shared the wonderful news of Christ's birth with the shepherds.

The angels delivered this message: "Fear not: for, behold, I bring you good tidings of great joy, which shall be to all people. For unto you is born this day in the city of David a Saviour, which is Christ the Lord," (Luke 2:10-11). Miraculous news.

The long-awaited Messiah was finally here. After the shepherds witnessed the new-born babe with their own eyes, they couldn't contain their joy. They rejoiced and told everyone about the Savior's birth.

Write about a time when you felt compelled to praise the Lord for something He did in your life: _____

_____

A Life Lesson:

The initial excitement had worn off. Starting a business had seemed like a good idea. A few months into it, I was having second thoughts. With no money coming in and bills piling up, I had no idea how things would turn out.

My husband Steve had a knack for technology. I had encouraged him to branch out and begin a business – Applied Logix. At least one company had shown interest in the customized software he was selling. Some income was better than none.

Following a successful software installation at Monster.com, we prayed for more companies to show interest. When another company requested a meeting, I remember praying for my husband to have another sale.

Steve called me when his plane touched down in Columbus, Ohio. The meeting had gone well. I had a hard time containing the excitement I felt as I drove the sixty-something miles from our house to the airport. I was pretty sure the company Steve had met with would eventually make a purchase.

When Steve shared the details of his meeting with CMD Group, I realized our prayer request had been answered. But not in the way we had imagined. The company was not only interested in the software, they were interested in buying our business. I was shocked.

I recognized my limited vision. God was in control of the situation the entire time. He knew what He was doing. His answer to our prayer was far better than my solutions. There was joy in knowing that the Lord had been walking with us through the entire experience and had provided miraculously for us.

What an opportunity to praise Him. It was definitely not something we had done. His fingerprints were evident on the entire string of events. Words of praise and thanksgiving were definitely in order: "I will bless the Lord at all times: his praise shall continually be in my mouth. My soul shall make her boast in the Lord: the humble shall hear thereof, and be glad. O magnify the Lord with me, and let us exalt his name together," (Psalm 34:1-3).

Over the years, the Lord has allowed Steve and me to share this story of encouragement with others. Experiencing God's care for us in the everyday things brings great joy. A joy that overflows into praise.

Write a prayer thanking the Lord for His everyday provisions:_____

_____

_____

A Word from God's Word:

Throngs of people bustled past him. What would it be like to walk? He had been lame since birth, and could only imagine how it would feel to navigate from one place to another on sturdy legs. As it was, he was forced to rely on others to carry him to the place he now sat.

He was a familiar fixture by the gate in front of the temple. Everyone was used to seeing him in this spot – doing the only thing he could do to survive: beg. Occasionally someone would have compassion on him and drop a coin in his cup. But lately, those going into the temple seemed to look right past him and avoid eye contact.

He held out his cup and asked for some money from two men passing by on their way to prayer. He wasn't ready for their response: "And Peter, fastening his eyes upon him with John, said, Look on us," (Acts 3:4). This was new. The majority of people acted as if they hadn't heard him, and merely went on their way. These men actually wanted his attention.

With eager anticipation, he held his cup up a bit higher; expecting the men to drop in a few coins. But the man was talking again: "Silver and gold have I none; but such as I have give I thee: In the name of Jesus Christ of Nazareth rise up and walk," (Acts 3:6).

Walk? The man was reaching down and grasping his hand. As he felt himself being lifted from the ground, something happened. His feet and ankle bones felt different. They felt strong. He could stand!

One moment he was seated on the ground begging, and the next he was standing on his own two feet. It was a miracle. He began walking and leaping and praising God (Acts 3:8). He was unable to contain the joy he felt.

Having the ability to walk changed his entire future. He'd be able to work. He'd no longer be a burden on society.

He'd asked the men for money that would sustain him for a day or two, and in return, they'd given him a new lease on life – strong legs that would be able to carry him to a job that would sustain him in the coming years.

As he ran joyfully into the temple with Peter and John, he knew it wasn't the men who had healed him. Only the power of Jesus Christ could perform such a miracle. God had healed him. And he lifted his voice in praise to the Lord.

The result of his joy turned into rejoicing. How did those around him respond? "...many of them which heard the word believed; and the number of the men was about five thousand," (Acts 4:4).

Write Psalm 86:10-12 in the space provided: _____

_____

_____

_____

When the joy of the Lord fills your life praise is the natural outcome. Magnify the Lord and allow Him to touch the hearts of those around you.

A Time to Reflect:

Does your joy overflow into praise? How does the Lord want you to respond today?_____

_____

_____

Prayer: *Heavenly Father, when I reflect on who You are and all You do, I'm filled with joy. Forgive me when I take You for granted. Help my joy to overflow into praise, so others will hear about Your greatness. In Jesus' name, Amen.*

Questions for Group Discussion:

1. What is the difference between joy and happiness?

2. What happened as a result of God's miraculous deliverance of His people and their joyful celebration? (Esther 8:16-17)

3. Difficult circumstances can be challenging. How was the widow referenced in 1 Kings 17 able to maintain her joy?

4. Have you experienced opposition while doing something for the Lord? How did He provide for you?

5. How do you think the miracle in Acts 3:1-8 changed the lame man's life? Spend some time in prayer, praising God for all He's done in your life.

Week 3

A Different Kind of Peace

Peace isn't only experienced in the absence of conflict. This week's lessons will detail how you can have the peace of God even in the midst of great turmoil. God's Word challenges believers to replace worrying with prayer and thanksgiving (Philippians 4:6). Each lesson will equip you with the truth necessary to cultivate peace in your life.

This week at a glance:

Day 1 – *A Major Purchase*

Day 2 – *Taming the Worry Monster*

Day 3 – *Nature Obeys*

Day 4 – *Harmony Can Happen*

Day 5 – *When the Going Gets Tough*

Day 1

A Major Purchase

A Moment to Meditate & Memorize:

Read and study this week's verse.

Colossians 3:15 *And let the peace of God rule in your hearts, to the which also ye are called in one body; and be ye thankful.*

Throughout history, man has sought peace with God. Unfortunately, man's solutions don't work. Peace is NOT something that can be earned. So how is it possible to experience peace with a holy God? God's way.

Today, let's discover the truth in God's Word.

Have you ever attempted to make peace with God your way? _____

_____

A Life Lesson:

They were different. I noticed it the first time they visited. A couple students from the college I attended had stopped by to conduct a survey. The topic of the survey? God and the Bible. While I had nothing against the subject matter, I couldn't understand why students would voluntarily spend their free time talking to people about Jesus.

One of my roommates and I took a few minutes to fill out the survey. I had been raised in church and was familiar with the Bible – so I wasn't surprised that I knew all the answers to the questions. Yet I was intrigued by these students who had an obvious passion for the Lord; something I couldn't claim. What was missing?

I began attending their weekly Bible study on campus, and met more people who were excited about God's Word and sharing it with others. When it came to discussing the verses, I was quick to let everyone know that I was familiar with these stories. While our scriptural knowledge may have been the same, I still couldn't place a finger on what was different about these students.

Several months later, a drama team came to our town performing a play entitled, "Heaven's Gates and Hell's Flames." It sounded interesting. As my friend and I entered the auditorium, we took our seats mid-way back from the stage.

The lights dimmed and the actors took their places. The opening scene depicted characters involved in everyday activities – but unexpected tragedies left each one dead. Immediately each character was either in heaven or hell. The drama team clearly illustrated what determined each performer's eternal fate. Heaven awaited the person who had believed in Jesus Christ as his/her personal Savior. Hell was the destination for the person who failed to place his/her faith in Christ during life on earth.

What had puzzled me for months became clear as the drama team enacted one scene after another. Knowing the facts about who Jesus was and what He had done was NOT what would get me to heaven. I had to realize my sinful condition and accept Jesus' sacrificial death on the cross as payment for my sin debt. By faith I believed – I bowed my head and called out to the Savior (Romans 10:13).

Now I understood what I had been missing: a reconciled relationship with God. A relationship that brought true peace.

Have you experienced peace with God? If so, tell your story:_____

_____

_____

_____

A Word from God's Word:

Imagine living in another time period. A time of sacrifices and offerings. The smell of burnt animal flesh and smoke: a constant reminder of the sin that separates you from your God.

The children of Israel were no strangers to this system. Moses had given them clear instructions for each of the offerings. Two of them were required: the sin offering and the trespass offering. The other three were voluntary, including the peace offering.

The mandatory offerings restored the sinner to fellowship with God, made payment to the injured parties, and reminded each person of the seriousness of sin. Once these offerings were made, the Israelite would often sacrifice a peace offering as well. It was a way to show gratitude to God, and symbolized peace and fellowship with Him (Life Application Study Bible, chart, p. 181).

It's hard to understand how sinful human beings can have peace with a holy God. The sacrifices offered by the priests on behalf of the Jewish people in the Old Testament, foreshadowed what was to come. The sinless Lamb of God would give Himself as a sacrifice in payment for all mankind's sin debt.

The apostle Paul beautifully described the transaction that was made to restore peace between God and man: "19 For it pleased the Father that in him (*Christ*) should all fulness dwell; 20 And, having made peace through the blood of his cross, by him to reconcile all things unto himself; by him, I say, whether they be things in earth, or things in heaven. 21 And you, that were some time alienated and enemies in your mind by wicked works, yet now hath he reconciled 22 In the body of his flesh through death, to present you holy and unblameable and unreproveable in his sight," (Colossians 1:19-22; words in italics mine).

Who purchased our peace?_____

Christ was the one who purchased our peace. A major purchase. Peace is now possible between man and God. The book of Ephesians gives the details: "But now in Christ Jesus ye who sometimes were far off are made nigh by the blood of Christ. For he is our peace, who hath made both (*Jews and Gentiles*) one, and hath broken down the middle wall of partition between us;" (Ephesians 2:13-14; words in italics mine).

Is there peace between you and God?_____

If not, there can be. Admit you are a sinner (Romans 3:23). Understand there is a penalty for your sins - eternal separation from God (Romans 6:23). Know that Christ paid the penalty for your sin debt when He died on the cross (Romans 5:8). Put your faith in the completed work of Christ, and call on Him to save you (Romans 10:13).

Experience peace between you and God today!

A Time to Reflect:

How does the Lord want you to respond to what He showed you today?_____

_____

_____

_____

Prayer: Heavenly Father, thank You for making a way for me to experience peace with You. Thank You for sending Your Son to be the ultimate sacrifice to pay my sin debt. Give me boldness to share the good news of salvation and Your peace with someone today. In Jesus' name, Amen.

Day 2

Taming the Worry Monster

A Moment to Meditate & Memorize:

Begin memorizing this week's verse.

Colossians 3:15 *And let the peace of God rule in your hearts, to the which also ye are called in one body; and be ye thankful.*

Human beings have a tendency to worry. What will happen if I lose my job? What if my spouse leaves? What if I'm diagnosed with cancer? The "what ifs" are endless. And does worrying accomplish anything?

Nothing productive. So why do we sign up for Worrying 101 when all it delivers are sleepless nights, ulcers, and headaches?

Today we'll discover how to experience God's peace even when worry comes calling.

A Life Lesson:

The situation made me uncomfortable. My Mom had been the picture of health as long as I could remember, yet now she was experiencing high blood pressure and ringing in her left ear. My Mom who had seemed self-sufficient through previous difficulties now needed my help. I felt the grip of anxiety tighten.

I packed enough clothes and toiletry items for a week, unsure how long I would need to stay. Sleep had eluded me the previous night, but I loaded my suitcase in the trunk and slid behind the wheel. Fatigue and the fact that I had never made the fourteen hour trip by myself, left me dreading the drive.

With my husband by my side, I would have been fine. We had made this trip numerous times. His strength would enable me to encourage my Mom, and help her wade through medical information to determine the best course of action. But he was unable to take a week off from work. This time I was alone.

As I drove, I was aware that my breathing was shallow and a tingling sensation was making its way down my arms. Fear was getting the best of me. I tried to concentrate on the CD that was playing, but my mind began to wander. What if my Mom had heart problems? I knew she wasn't getting much sleep, and was having a hard time maintaining her normal schedule. What if she had to have surgery? It was difficult to imagine my Mom being anything other than the rock-solid woman I had known all my life.

Doctor's appointments and medical tests shed little light on her condition. The good news? Her heart seemed strong and healthy. The bad news? No one could put a finger on what was causing the high blood pressure, or the ringing in her ear. Medication only seemed to help for a day or two before it caused uncomfortable side effects. With few answers and no end in sight, I tried to divert my Mom's attention while fighting my own anxiety.

Worrying was getting me nowhere. In fact, it was counterproductive. As I cried out to the Lord, His Word gave me the strength and peace I needed. Jesus' clear teaching echoed from my Bible: *"25 Therefore I say unto you, Take no thought for your life, what ye shall eat, or what ye shall drink; nor yet for your body, what ye shall put on. Is not the life more than meat, and the body than raiment? 26 Behold the fowls of the air: for they sow not, neither do they reap, nor gather into barns; yet your heavenly Father feedeth them. Are ye not much better than they?"* (Matthew 6:25-26).

The Lord loved me. His will for me was to trust Him. He would provide for my Mom's needs as well as my own. I remembered numerous times He had done just that, and decided to take a step of faith. As I cast my cares on Him, He did indeed care for me (1 Peter 5:7). My anxiety dissipated and God's peace settled in its place.

Do you have a tendency to worry? Write about a time when the Lord provided for you:_____

_____

_____

A Word from God's Word:

The children of Israel had witnessed the mighty hand of God at work. Numerous plagues had tormented the Egyptians, affecting everything from drinking water to food. The final plague, death of all the firstborn, convinced Pharaoh to let the Israelites go. They were free at last! Unbelievable to think that they had been slaves just hours before, and now Pharaoh was begging them to leave.

But their excitement was short-lived. As they camped by the Red Sea, fear set in - they could see dust clouds on the horizon indicating that a large group was approaching. It could only mean one thing: Pharaoh and his armies had come after them to bring them into bondage once again. They were trapped.

With no escape route in sight the Israelites cried out to the Lord, and quickly turned on Moses. Why had he brought them out into the wilderness to die? Hadn't they told him it would be better for them to serve the Egyptians than to die out here in the wasteland? (Exodus 14:11-12) Once they were captured, Pharaoh would punish them and make their return to slavery unbearable.

Moses' words silenced the people: "Fear ye not, stand still, and see the salvation of the Lord, which he will show to you today: for the Egyptians whom ye have seen today, ye shall see them again no more for ever," (Exodus 14:13).

Who was going to fight for the Israelites (Exodus 14:14)?_____

_____

The people had to be dumbfounded. Really? The Lord was going to defeat the enemy? And the Israelites wouldn't even have to fight?

It sounded too good to be true. But with dusk closing in something was happening. The pillar of cloud that led them during the day had shifted to a position behind them – preventing the enemy from overtaking them. And Moses was stretching out his hand over the Red Sea (Exodus 14:21). This was how the Lord was going to do it. He would provide them with a way of escape: THROUGH the Red Sea.

The wind began to blow and the sea parted. With walls of water on either side of them, the children of Israel walked through the middle of the sea. No need to worry about their sandals getting wet because the Lord had used the east wind to dry the sea floor.

Only one small concern. Wouldn't the Egyptians follow them? Sure enough. The Israelites could see the chariots of Pharaoh and his army entering the Red Sea. But the Lord had promised to fight for them, and He did. Pharaoh's army seemed unable to drive their chariots. Ground that had been dry for the Israelites was like quicksand to the Egyptians – chariot wheels were either submerged in sand or completely removed.

As the Israelites stood on the banks of the Red Sea and watched in amazement, Moses stretched out his hand once again and the walls of water came crashing down on the trapped Egyptians. Not one of their enemies survived (Exodus 14:28).

How did the Israelites respond to the miracle the Lord performed (Exodus 14:31)?_____

_____

The people believed in and feared the Lord and His servant Moses. When plagued by fear Moses reminded the Israelites to stand still and look to the Lord for deliverance. Fear was replaced by faith and the people were able to experience peace.

The same is true in our lives. Instead of being paralyzed by fear, choose to trust God in those difficult times and He will provide peace.

A Time to Reflect:

Does fear or faith characterize your response to difficulties? How does the Lord want you to respond today?_____

_____

_____

Prayer: Heavenly Father, thank You for working in my life. I realize difficulties are opportunities to grow in faith and experience Your peace. Help me to remember all the times You've delivered me in the past. Give me strength to choose faith over fear. In Jesus' name, Amen.

Day 3

Nature Obeys

A Moment to Meditate & Memorize:

Continue memorizing this week's verse.

Colossians 3:15 *And let the peace of God rule in your hearts, to the which also ye are called in one body; and be ye thankful.*

Storms can be scary. Weather alarms and instant messaging have done much in the way of helping us prepare for adverse conditions. When bad weather strikes, how do you handle it?

There can be peace in the midst of the storm when you know the Creator of the universe!

A Life Lesson:

The storm seemed to be chasing us. Our vacation had been cut short due to the arrival of Hurricane Ivan. The threat from this storm had caused a mandatory evacuation from the condominiums where we were staying. We spent the night on the road with countless other travelers, determined to leave the storm as far behind as possible.

Our home was a welcome sight after driving all night long. With beds beckoning, we didn't give the leaden-grey skies much thought. Later that day, however, the weather channel confirmed our growing suspicions – Hurricane Ivan, which had unleashed massive damage in the Florida panhandle, was now a tropical storm heading straight for us. We could expect high winds and torrential downpours over the next 48 hours.

A trip to the grocery story was a must. With bags of food filling the trunk, we drove the few miles home increasingly aware of the storm brewing outside. With the wind picking up speed, we drove into the garage and unloaded our groceries as quickly as possible. The sky opened up and the deluge began.

With thunder rolling and rain pelting the roof, we detected a sound unlike any other – a mighty groaning accompanied by snapping and sighing. The sound gave way to a quake that shook the ground. An enormous oak tree that had once stood like a sentinel was now lying across the driveway we had just driven up moments before.

As we closed our garage door on the sight of the downed oak, I realized how fortunate we were. The tree hadn't fallen when we were in the driveway, and it had narrowly missed the front corner of our house. The Lord had protected us.

As the rain continued to descend in buckets, and the wind howled with abandon, we glanced with increasing concern at several humongous trees that seemed to be much closer to the house than they had the previous day. Two trees in particular were especially worrisome. If either of them were uprooted, we would be in serious danger.

We heard the ominous sound again. Felt the vibration. We ran to the front of the house and witnessed an exposed root ball that stood nearly twelve feet tall.

Another grand oak, over 100 feet in height, had crashed to the ground. Once again we had been spared.

In the space of a few minutes, we had lost two huge, sturdy oak trees. Prayers that had been sent up silently were now spoken aloud: "Thank you for protecting us Lord. We're so thankful the trees fell without harming anyone or anything. Just like Your Word says, 'What time I am afraid, I will trust in thee,'" (Psalm 56:3).

The storm continued to rage the rest of the day and into the night. The saturated ground and the strong winds created potential for tremendous damage. But within the walls of our home, my family and I experienced peace. We knew the One who had protected us – the One who could calm every storm.

Write about a time when the Lord gave you peace in the middle of a storm:_

_____

_____

A Word from God's Word:

Have you ever been on the lake or ocean when a storm is brewing? There's just something about large, menacing clouds and rolling, angry waves that make a person feel small and helpless. Even experienced fishermen know when a storm is more than they can handle.

It probably began like any other day. The disciples had followed Jesus to the seaside and soon a crowd had gathered. They wanted to hear Jesus teach. Before long Jesus had to step into one of the boats on shore and row a few feet out to avoid the press of the multitude. His parables captured their attention.

Time passed and still He taught. Finally it became necessary for Jesus to dismiss the crowd. He then explained the parables in greater detail to the twelve disciples. The sun was slipping behind the clouds on the horizon, when Jesus suggested they sail the boat to the other side of the lake.

A journey the seasoned fishermen had made too many times to count, suddenly became frightening. One minute the sea was smooth as glass, the next minute, gale force winds pummeled the craft, causing the ship to take on water. The disciples did everything in their power to bail the boat: to no avail. Never had they encountered such a storm. Without help their boat would sink.

Jesus. Surely He could help them. But where was He? In the tumult of the storm, and in doing all they could to keep their boat afloat, the disciples had lost track of their Master. He was still in the back of the boat. What was He doing? Sleeping? How could He sleep at a time like this?

Fear was evident in the voices of the disciples as they woke Jesus. Didn't He care about them? They would all die at sea if He didn't do something at once. As He stood, He rebuked the wind, and when He spoke to the sea it was impossible to miss the authority in His voice: "Peace, be still," (Mark 4:39). Immediately, the wind stopped and the sea became calm once again.

What simple question did Jesus ask the disciples (Mark 4:40)?_____

_____

_____

Why didn't they have faith in Him? They tried overcoming the power of the storm using their strength and intelligence. What was the result? A boat that nearly capsized. Only when they realized the storm was more than they could handle did they turn to Jesus. Shouldn't they have turned to Him first? He was the Lord of creation. And He had proven it: even the wind and the sea were at His command.

Are you quick to lean on your own expertise when things get rough? Learn a lesson from the disciples and turn to Jesus at the first sign of difficulty. You'll be sure to experience His peace.

A Time to Reflect:

How does the Lord want you to respond to the lesson today?_____

_____

_____

Prayer: Heavenly Father, thank You for being the Lord of creation. When storms come, I know You are still in control. Help me to turn to You at the first sign of difficulty. Strengthen my faith. In Jesus' name, Amen.

Day 4

Harmony Can Happen

A Moment to Meditate & Memorize:

Continue memorizing this week's verse.

Colossians 3:15 *And let the peace of God rule in your hearts, to the which also ye are called in one body; and be ye thankful.*

Peace can be an abstract concept. But when we think about peace in terms of unity among family members and believers, it's a concept that touches each of us where we live.

Striving for peace on our own often ends in disaster. Today's lesson reveals some keys to cultivating peace God's way.

Take a few moments to read and think about 1 Peter 3:10-11 (word in parentheses mine):

For he that will love life, and see good days, let him refrain his tongue from evil, and his lips that they speak no guile: Let him eschew evil, and do good; let him seek peace, and ensue (pursue) it.

A Life Lesson:

The incident happened more than three decades ago – yet I remember it clearly. My family and I were visiting my grandparents in New Port Richey, Florida. Christmastime for our household consisted of an annual trip to the sunshine state to celebrate the holiday with my Dad's parents.

As kids, my brother and I thoroughly enjoyed every minute of the trip including the drive. We'd let our imaginations run wild as we would create elaborate plots for our stuffed monkeys to execute – completely oblivious to the scenery rushing by our windows. On this particular trip, it was probably my overactive imagination that got me into trouble.

When we arrived there were hugs all around, and my brother and I made a beeline for our favorite room in the house: the Florida room; complete with louvered windows and a sliding glass door. Not only did the room serve as our makeshift bedroom during our stay, but it was the site of countless adventures for our sock monkey friends.

The next morning after reenacting a daring quest, in which the monkeys narrowly escaped from the bad guys, it was time to put our imaginations on hold and get back to reality. Following an early lunch, my parents, grandparents, brother, and I climbed into the car for a shopping trip. I must have dozed off on the way to the store, because the next thing I remember was my grandma gently shaking me awake.

I'm not sure what possessed me to say it – maybe I was still caught up in the imaginary plot with the evil men. For whatever reason, I managed to look at my grandma and say, "Grandma, you're a dirty rug." From the look on her face, I knew I'd deeply offended and angered her. Her words confirmed it: "You can say that about your friends, but don't you ever call me a dirty rug."

A lie tumbled from my lips: "I didn't say you were a dirty rug. I said **I** was a dirty rug." Recognizing the falsehood for what it was, my grandma just shook her head. I had been rude and disrespectful and had caused conflict in our family.

What should I do? There was only one thing to do. Apologize. Although I don't remember exactly what I said, I know my grandma forgave me and harmony was restored between us.

I can appreciate the words of the Psalmist David: "Behold, how good and how pleasant it is for brethren to dwell together in unity," (Psalms 133:1). Whether referring to brothers and sisters in Christ or to family members, the truth remains – unity creates peace.

Write about a time you created conflict. How was peace restored?_____

_____

_____

A Word from God's Word:

Of all places you'd expect unity, the church would top the list, right? Unfortunately, throughout history the church has dealt with its fair share of conflict. Conflict among its members.

The apostle Paul was no stranger to conflict. Nor did he have a problem dealing with it. He was well acquainted with human nature and was used to addressing sin directly. On every missionary journey he established churches and taught the gospel. When he moved on, he stayed in contact with each church tracking the member's progress – exhorting and encouraging them through letters.

Paul had heard from various sources that the church in Corinth was struggling. Jealousy and divisiveness were among the main issues. Conflict abounded. I can imagine Paul praying fervently before putting pen to parchment to address these concerns.

A greeting was quickly scrawled and then he got right to the point: "Now I beseech you, brethren, by the name of our Lord Jesus Christ, that ye all speak the same thing, and that there be no divisions among you; but that ye be perfectly joined together in the same mind and in the same judgment," (1 Corinthians 1:10).

These believers were pitted in arguments about which preacher was superior. Some preferred Paul, others Apollos, and some Cephas.

Seems like a trivial argument, right? But the same thing happens today. Jealousies arise over whose preacher is the best. Is Christ being preached? If so, focus on magnifying Christ.

Because of the conflict that abounded in the Corinthian church, Paul had to reiterate the basics to these believers. No doubt about it, they were acting like children. They needed a reminder.

Write out 1 Corithians 3:7_____

_____

Each believer played a part in the body of Christ, but God was to receive the glory for all that was accomplished.

Paul cautioned these Christians to remember the God who created them and the Holy Spirit who indwelt them (1 Corinthians 3:16). Any ability a man or woman possessed was a gift from the Lord. As a result, no one had the right to boast. (1 Corinthians 4:7).

Just as in Paul's day, unbelievers find little reason to join our ranks when bickering and dissension fill our churches. In a different letter to the Philippians, Paul shares a key to unity, "3 Let nothing be done through strife or vainglory; but in lowliness of mind let each esteem other better than themselves. 4 Look not every man on his own things, but every man also on the things of others," (Philippians 2:3-4).

When we choose to practice the mind of Christ, we humble ourselves out of concern for one another, and God is glorified. There's something powerful and magnetic about a group of believers willing to become selfless in order to point to the Prince of Peace – Jesus. The outcome? Unity and peace.

A Time to Reflect:

How does the Lord want you to respond to the lesson today?_____

_____

_____

Prayer: Heavenly Father, thank You for reminding me of the importance of unity. Forgive me when I create conflict. Help me to choose to think like You - to serve others and make much of Jesus. When I do, I know I'll experience Your peace. In Jesus' name, Amen.

Day 5

When the Going Gets Tough

A Moment to Meditate & Memorize:

Finish memorizing this week's verse.

Colossians 3:15 *And let the peace of God rule in your hearts, to the which also ye are called in one body; and be ye thankful.*

When things don't go the way you expect them to, do you experience anxiety or peace? For the child of God, peace is available.

Today we'll look at the kind of peace that goes beyond an absence of conflict – a very real peace the Lord intended for each one of us to enjoy.

We've studied this fruit of the Spirit in the previous four lessons. How would you define "peace"?_____

_____

Peace: freedom from war; tranquility - a calm and quiet state, free from disturbances or noise; mental calm - a state of mental calm and serenity, with no anxiety; harmony - freedom from conflict or disagreement among people or groups of people.(Encarta Dictionary)

A Life Lesson:

The call was unexpected. My husband answered the phone. I don't remember what he said, but from his response I could tell something was terribly wrong. He passed me the phone, concern etched on his face.

Before my Mom spoke, I knew my Dad had passed away. Her words confirmed my fear. He had suffered with severe rheumatoid arthritis and heart problems for years. We were supposed to make the trip up to Michigan to celebrate Christmas together. Instead, we'd be travelling up for his funeral.

I had attended many funerals. And it always amazed me that people who had experienced devastating loss could continue to function in spite of their grief. The most vivid example was the mother who lost one teenage daughter in a horrific car accident, while her other daughter was sped to the hospital with serious injuries. Days later, she wrote about the wonderful celebration service they had for her oldest daughter who was now in heaven.

Throughout her youngest daughter's slow journey to recovery, this mother journaled about the experience and refused to be filled with anxiety. In a matter of seconds her world was turned upside down. Things would never be the same for her family. I'm sure she went through periods of intense sadness and wondered why this tragedy happened – yet the peace of God was evident in the written updates she shared.

As I hung up the phone following my Mom's call, it was my turn to experience the peace of God. I could sense the Lord's presence as the Holy Spirit reminded me of Bible verses I had memorized years before: "Thou wilt keep him in perfect peace, whose mind is stayed on thee: because he trusteth in thee. Trust ye in the Lord for ever: for in the Lord Jehovah is everlasting strength," (Isaiah 26:3-4). Comforting words of hope.

In spite of heartache and loss, the Lord's peace gave me hope. Would there be difficult days ahead? Absolutely. But moment by moment, as I gave my worries and concerns to the Lord, He was true to His Word: "6 Be careful for nothing; but in every thing by prayer and supplication with thanksgiving let your requests be made known unto God. 7 And the peace of God, which passeth all understanding, shall keep your hearts and minds through Christ Jesus," (Philippians 4:6-7).

As I surrendered my anxiety and care to the Lord, He provided exactly what I needed: His peace.

Write about a time you experienced the peace of God:_____

_____

_____

A Word from God's Word:

They had spent three and a half years with Him. They had heard Him preach. Listened to Him explain parables. And had witnessed miracles performed by His hands. Yet in spite of all this, the disciples still had much to learn of Jesus Christ the Messiah.

Some of the disciples expected Jesus to set up an earthly kingdom. He had a large following, and they had been there when He'd turned five loaves of bread and two small fish into enough food to feed a crowd of more than five thousand people. Surely Jesus was able to overthrow the Roman government of the day.

His words had been plain.

Write out Matthew 10:34:_____

_____

_____

That **must** mean Jesus was preparing a takeover. But recently, He'd been talking about going away. It didn't make sense.

After the morning discussion, Judas (not Judas Iscariot) had been bold enough to ask the question that was on all of their minds. Why wouldn't Jesus announce to the world that He was the Messiah? (John 14:22) They listened intently to Jesus' response.

He explained that not everyone could understand His message. But soon the Holy Spirit would be sent to help the disciples remember what Jesus had said. The disciples would be entrusted with sharing the gospel with the world.

Who was Jesus going to send to help them after He left? (John 14:26)_____

_____

He continued speaking, clarifying his mission, *"27 Peace I leave with you, my peace I give unto you: not as the world giveth, give I unto you. Let not your heart be troubled, neither let it be afraid. 28 Ye have heard how I said unto you, I go away, and come again unto you. If ye loved me, ye would rejoice, because I said, I go unto the Father: for my Father is greater than I."* (John 14:27-28).

The peace He mentioned sounded unlike any peace the disciples were familiar with. Even though they still didn't understand completely each of the disciples was faced with a decision. Would they trust Christ and the words He spoke, or would they continue to try to fit Christ into a mold of their making?

The disciples' decisions were evident following Jesus' crucifixion and resurrection. Although they struggled with doubts they chose to trust Christ and were filled with the Holy Ghost (Acts 2:1-4). They became bold witnesses who shared the gospel with Jews and Gentiles alike. And despite persecution, they experienced the peace of God.

A Time to Reflect:

Do you typically equate peace with an absence of conflict? How does the Lord want you to respond to what He showed you today?_____

_____

_____

Prayer: Heavenly Father, thank You for Your peace that passes understanding. I can experience Your peace in spite of my circumstances because of the presence of Your Holy Spirit. Help the fruit of peace to grow in my life today. In Jesus' name, Amen.

Questions for Group Discussion:

1. How is it possible for man to have peace with a holy God? Do you have this peace?

2. We all face fear. How can we be victorious over the temptation to worry?

3. Time for a faith check-up. When faced with life's storms what statement best describes you:

    * I try to figure out the best way to handle it

    * I turn to family and friends for advice

    * I ask God to help me

    * I freeze in fear

4. According to Philippians 2:3-4, how is it possible to have unity in the body of believers?

5. Read Philippians 4:6-7. How can you experience the peace of God which passes all understanding?

Hang in There: The Art of Suffering Long

No one enjoys trials. When they are prolonged, it becomes even more difficult to choose the right attitude day after day. But, as a result of hardships, we do have the opportunity to develop a characteristic that can be acquired no other way: longsuffering. Does the concept of patient endurance in the face of suffering come naturally? Absolutely not - but this week we'll take a look at how embracing our trials as part of God's perfect will, can help us develop this important fruit of the Spirit.

This week at a glance:

Day 1 – *More Questions than Answers*

Day 2 – *Going Beyond*

Day 3 – *Passionate Pursuit*

Day 4 – *A Perspective that Pleases*

Day 5 – *Years of Patience*

Day 1

More Questions than Answers

A Moment to Meditate & Memorize:

This week we'll discover the nature of a longsuffering spirit. Read and study our verse:

Psalm 86:15 But thou, O Lord, art a God full of compassion, and gracious, longsuffering, and plenteous in mercy and truth.

Longsuffering. Although we don't use this word in everyday conversation, it means exactly what it says - to suffer long. Spelled out in a definition, this trait would be defined as "patient and enduring in the face of suffering or difficulty," (Encarta Dictionary).

Longsuffering is listed as the fourth characteristic of the fruit of the Spirit. By submitting to the control of the Holy Spirit, it's possible to put up with unfavorable circumstances for an extended period of time. The result? Others will see a difference in our response and we'll be able to point them to the Savior.

Write about a time when you were longsuffering:_____

_____

_____

A Life Lesson:

It hadn't happened before. Previous years had begun without a specified quota, but within a month or two of the first quarter, a product set was assigned, and the quota was established. Not so this year. Moving into mid-April, the only thing that was clear was change. And lots of it. My husband Steve's company seemed to be in the process of a major re-organization.

With change came questions. Who would he report to this year? What would his responsibilities involve? Which accounts would he cover? Would his schedule continue to include extensive travel? So many questions. Questions he was unable to answer.

Although there were more questions than answers, I watched my husband adjust to the stress of the unknowns. Still fulfilling the obligations he had since the beginning of the year, he continued to function moment by moment, one day at a time.

It was frustrating to know there was nothing I could do to change the situation. But I could continue to be supportive of my husband, make sure he had everything he needed prior to traveling, and pray for him. Difficult circumstances in the past had always proven to be opportunities to trust the Lord. This was no exception.

Stress could easily take a toll. Although the weeks passed with few answers, Steve continued to do what was required of him as if everything was normal. Customer meetings, speaking engagements, endless conference calls. Still no answers.

I admired his determination to do what was right. It would have been easy to let frustration get the upper hand, grumble and complain, and begin looking for another job. But instead of giving in to pride, my husband chose to believe the Lord had a plan, and just kept up with the hectic pace that his present job demanded. He chose to be patient and enduring in the face of difficulty. He chose to be longsuffering.

Trials of life allow opportunities for growth. As the Apostle Paul so aptly put it, "For whom he did foreknow, he also did predestinate to be conformed to the image of his Son..." (Romans 8:29). Each difficulty gives us a chance to trust the Lord with our circumstance, and leave it in His capable hands. And when we do, the Holy Spirit is able to produce something that's pleasing to Him – the fruit of longsuffering.

How do you respond when you're faced with more questions than answers?_

_____

_____

A Word from God's Word:

His coat of many colors made it obvious - Joseph was the favorite son. Tension grew between siblings and hatred followed. It was impossible to discuss anything without arguing. His dreams were driving them crazy. Who did he think he was telling them that one day they would bow down before him? Something had to be done about Joseph.

On an errand for his father, Joseph went to check on his brothers and their sheep. His brothers weren't in the mood for a visitor – especially one wearing an all-too-familiar multi-colored coat. They recognized Joseph from a distance and formulated a plan to kill him (Genesis 37:18).

What did the brothers do with Joseph? (Genesis 37:28)_____

_____

_____

Joseph was sold to the Midianites and eventually became a slave to Potiphar, one of Pharaoh's officers. Alone, in a foreign land, Joseph knew the Lord was still with him. God gave him favor with his master and Joseph was made overseer of everything in Potiphar's house. Maybe things were looking up.

Potiphar's wife had taken notice of Joseph too, but she wasn't interested in his godly work ethic. Her words to Joseph betrayed her intent, "Lie with me," (Genesis 39:7). Day after day, she tried to entice him, but with each advance, Joseph chose to retreat.

Fed up with his refusal of her invitations, what did Potiphar's wife say about Joseph? (Genesis 39:14-15) _____

_____

Although innocent of her accusation, Joseph found himself staring at the walls of a prison.

What was happening? First he was sold into slavery. Now prison was his reward for fleeing temptation and doing the right thing. "But the Lord was with Joseph, and shewed him mercy, and gave him favour in the sight of the keeper of the prison," (Genesis 39:21). God was at work.

Joseph was put in charge of all the prisoners because the keeper saw that the Lord was with Joseph, and made everything he did to prosper. When Pharaoh's butler and baker ended up in prison, it was Joseph who took care of their needs. Little did he know one of those needs would be interpreting their dreams.

The morning following their strange dreams, the butler and baker were distraught. When Joseph asked them why they were so upset, they told him about their confusing dreams. Joseph was quick to share his faith that God could help them, "Do not interpretations belong to God?" (Genesis 40:8b). With the help of the Lord, Joseph accurately interpreted both dreams: in three days, the chief baker was hung, and the chief butler was restored to his position in Pharaoh's household.

Before the butler returned to his job, what was Joseph's request? (Genesis 40:14-15) _____

_____

Such a small request. But the butler forgot all about Joseph.

Two years later, Pharaoh had a disturbing dream that none of his wise men could interpret. Finally the butler's memory kicked in, and he recalled the young Hebrew man who was able to accurately interpret his dream. Surely he would be able to help Pharaoh!

As quickly as he had been thrown into prison, Joseph was whisked into Pharaoh's presence. No one knew what Pharaoh's dream meant. Could he give the interpretation? Joseph determined to glorify God, "It is not in me: God shall give Pharaoh an answer of peace," (Genesis 41:16). There would be seven years of abundant food in the land of Egypt, followed by seven years of severe famine. Filled with the wisdom of God, Joseph recommended appointing a leader to store up food during the years of plenty so there would be food during the many years of famine.

Who did Pharaoh appoint? Why? (Genesis 41:38-40)_____

_____

Pharaoh could see the spirit of the Lord in Joseph. Joseph endured extreme difficulty over the course of many years. He was: sold into slavery by his brothers, sent to prison for a crime he didn't commit, and forgotten for two years. Joseph chose to be longsuffering and yielded to God's will in spite of the injustice.

A Time to Reflect:

How does the Lord want you to respond to what He showed you today?_____

_____

_____

Prayer: Heavenly Father, thank You for the difficulties You allow me to experience. I realize they're necessary in order for longsuffering to be developed in my life. Help me to put up with unfavorable circumstances as long as I need to, so I can bring glory to You. In Jesus' name, Amen.

Day 2

Going Beyond

A Moment to Meditate & Memorize:

This week we're discovering the nature of a longsuffering spirit. Continue memorizing our verse:

Psalm 86:15 But thou, O Lord, art a God full of compassion, and gracious, longsuffering, and plenteous in mercy and truth.

Has there ever been a time when someone owed you something? Whether it's financial, service-related, or an apology, it's often difficult to demonstrate a longsuffering spirit when repayment isn't forthcoming. Today we'll see how these situations provide us with the opportunity to continue developing an attitude that patiently endures.

A Life Lesson:

The medical bills were adding up. Although auto insurance was covering the cost to repair our vehicle, the deductible still had to be paid. In a matter of seconds, a freak accident had placed me in this position. The police officer at the scene didn't issue tickets, but filed his report stating I was thirty percent at fault. The other driver and I were to file claims with our insurance companies.

That was the beginning of the waiting game – and I was not a happy participant. The accident happened on a holiday weekend, so I couldn't talk to a representative until the following week. Tuesday arrived, and I was highly motivated to get everything rolling.

A few strategically placed phone calls and things should be well on their way toward resolution – or so I thought. The reality? I discovered the driver of the other vehicle only carried the minimum amount of insurance on her vehicle, and her insurance company was not very reputable. When taken together, these facts pointed to a grim conclusion: it would take a long time to get reimbursed from her insurance company for anything.

I was angry. It was the principle of the situation. The other driver was seventy percent at fault for the accident, and yet I was required to pay one hundred percent of my bills. I wanted resolution and I wanted it immediately. But resolution didn't come, and the other party's insurance company refused to pay for expenses related to the accident. I have to admit I was anything but longsuffering.

An attorney, a court case, and three years later, I finally received a portion of my out of pocket expenses. It was over the course of that very long time that I learned to let the issue go, and see the value of choosing a longsuffering attitude. The Lord didn't remove me from the situation, but instead, He walked through it with me.

What are the benefits of being longsuffering?_____

_____

_____

A Word from God's Word:

It's a story of extremes – great joy followed by intense hatred. Paul and Barnabas had arrived in Lystra and begun preaching the gospel. They spoke with authority. People were listening. And now Paul was speaking loudly to the man who had been lame all his life, "Stand upright on thy feet," (Acts 14:10). Following the command, the former cripple leaped up and began walking.

The townspeople couldn't believe what they were seeing. It was a miracle. These visitors must be gods. "And they called Barnabas, Jupiter; and Paul, Mercurius, because he was the chief speaker," (Acts 14:12). It was only fitting that a sacrifice be made to these extraordinary gods.

When Paul and Barnabas learned of the people's intent, they begged the crowd not to worship them saying, "Sirs, why do ye these things? We also are men of like passions with you, and preach unto you that ye should turn from these vanities unto the living God, which made heaven, and earth, and the sea, and all things that are therein," (Acts 14:15). The people reluctantly accepted Paul and Barnabas' explanation. But real trouble was about to begin.

Several weeks earlier, Paul and Barnabas had been traveling in Iconium sharing the gospel of Christ. Whenever someone drew a crowd, there were always those who were jealous. It was no different for Paul and Barnabas. Many believed their testimony. But the unbelieving Jews caused such a stir that the city was divided – some agreed with the Jews, others agreed with the apostles.

What problem did this cause? (Acts 14:5)_____

_____

Those who were opposed to Paul and Barnabas wanted to stone them! When the apostles got wind of the plot, they fled to Lystra.

Determined to do away with the apostles, the unbelieving Jews followed them to Lystra. It didn't take much to convince the superstitious people of the town that Paul and Barnabas were imposters. The crowd who had been willing to worship the men only moments before, were now willing to take up rocks and stone the two.

What happened to Paul? (Acts 14:19)_____

_____

_____

Stoned and left for dead, Paul was taken outside of the city. But the story doesn't end there. Miraculously, Paul didn't die. He got up, and went back into the city! Instead of cursing those who had stoned him, Paul forgave them and continued to share the gospel with them. No mention is made of his attackers asking forgiveness.

Where did Paul go following his trip to Derbe?(Acts 14:21)_____

_____

Hard to believe Paul would return to Lystra, forgive his tormentors and demonstrate such a longsuffering attitude! But then again, that's the power of the Holy Spirit at work.

A Time to Reflect:

How does the Lord want you to respond to what He showed you today?_____

_____

_____

Prayer: *Heavenly Father, thank You for giving me concrete examples from Your Word, of a longsuffering attitude. Help me to see others through Your eyes of compassion. Give me the strength I need to choose to patiently endure today. In Jesus' name, Amen.*

Day 3

Passionate Pursuit

A Moment to Meditate & Memorize:

This week we're discovering the nature of a longsuffering spirit. Continue memorizing our verse:

Psalm 86:15 But thou, O Lord, art a God full of compassion, and gracious, longsuffering, and plenteous in mercy and truth.

I'll be the first to admit it - when I'm in the middle of a difficult situation; I look for the quickest way to escape. But oftentimes, instead of taking me out of the trial, the Lord teaches me how to walk through the trial with Him. In the process, He equips me to endure for the long haul.

A Life Lesson:

The car accident hadn't been severe. A small car had attempted to pass my SUV as I began navigating a turn. Instead of passing me, the driver sped into the side of my vehicle, driving both our vehicles off the road. A trip to the emergency room revealed some soft tissue injuries in my neck and back, but no broken bones.

While the physical pain slowly subsided, something unfamiliar took its place. Lack of sleep gave way to a gnawing fear I had never experienced – anxiety. My mind was in overdrive. I found it hard to process information, but I couldn't get my mind to shut off. Negativity dominated my thinking.

My husband Steve saw my suffering shift from physical to emotional. Neither one of us knew what was happening. Steve did his best to answer my questions. Unfortunately, my mind couldn't properly frame his responses and I'd repeat the same question three or four times. Without any sign of irritation, he would calmly explain the answer one more time.

As weeks turned into months, my husband did everything he could to help me sort out what I was going through. I witnessed his love when he canceled a meeting with a colleague at the last minute because I couldn't stand the thought of being alone. He accompanied me to doctors' appointments, bought me books that addressed coping with stress, and forfeited his own sleep in order to talk me through my irrational thinking. Over a period of time, with the help of family and friends, medicine, counseling, and the power of God's Word, healing came.

As I think back on that valley in my life, I am keenly aware of my husband's love. He embodied patience in a way that continues to challenge me. The apostle Paul uses the term, long-suffering when referring to this admirable trait. In fact, it's the first term in a string of words used to define love, or charity (1 Corinthians 13:4).

I am thankful to the Lord for my husband Steve - a living example of what it looks like to be longsuffering.

How will you exhibit this trait today?_____

_____

A Word from God's Word:

It's an unusual story. An entire book of the Bible is devoted to sharing Israel's sin and coming judgment. While this same theme is seen repeatedly in the Old Testament, in this account God chose a unique teaching tool to get His point across. He instructed His prophet, Hosea, to marry Gomer - a prostitute: not your typical directive.

What was Hosea's response? (Hosea 1:3)_____

Hosea obeyed. I can only imagine Hosea's relationship with Gomer. They were blessed with two children and things seemed to be going well. But as God's prophet, Hosea knew that just like Israel, Gomer would turn back to her adulterous ways.

The day probably began like so many others – a meal with the family before heading out to preach. No doubt Hosea encountered the same unreceptive crowd.

As he headed home, he may have reviewed the interesting stories he would share with his family that night at the evening meal. But as he opened the door, something was different. The place was strangely silent. His heart rate may have accelerated as he moved hastily from room to room. Gomer was gone. She had seemed a bit distant lately, and now she had left him for someone else.

The lesson was clear. Gomer's actions served as an example of Israel's unfaithfulness. Gomer had committed adultery of a physical nature, and by running after everything but God, Israel had committed spiritual adultery. God's great love for the people of Israel caused Him to warn them to repent and turn back to Him. He could not tolerate sin and if they continued on their current path, His judgment was sure to follow. His passionate pursuit of Israel is precious.

Write out Hosea 2:14:_____

_____

What were God's instructions for Hosea? Demonstrate the Lord's longsuffering nature and pursue his unfaithful wife. Once again, Hosea obeyed. How his heart must have broken as Gomer chose other lovers instead of him – still he pursued her.

God's response toward the nation of Israel was no different. He gave Hosea a picture of His love for the wayward people, "Go yet, love a woman beloved of her friend, yet an adulteress, according to the love of the Lord toward the children of Israel, who look to other gods, and love flagons of wine," (Hosea 3:1). In spite of Gomer's rejection and betrayal, Hosea was to buy her back.

What did Hosea do? (Hosea 3:2)_____

He continued to obey the Lord. By his obedience, Hosea was a living example of the longsuffering nature of God's love for His people. What was His promise for those who turned back to Him? "I will heal their backsliding, I will love them freely: for mine anger is turned away from him," (Hosea 14:4). Love suffers long!

A Time to Reflect:

*How has the Lord spoken to you about being longsuffering today?*_____

_____

_____

Prayer: *Heavenly Father, thank You for Your perfect love. Thank You for the picture of love You paint for me in Your Word, the Bible. Help me to walk in the power of the Holy Spirit, so I can love others selflessly with patient endurance. In Jesus' name, Amen.*

Day 4

A Perspective that Pleases

A Moment to Meditate & Memorize:

Continue memorizing the verse for this week:

Psalm 86:15 But thou, O Lord, art a God full of compassion, and gracious, longsuffering, and plenteous in mercy and truth.

There's often a warning that accompanies the prayer for patience – the Lord will answer by sending trials that will develop that very characteristic. Although I'm not eager to sign up for difficulties, I have to admit when I'm tested, there's always an opportunity for me to choose to grow in patience. The apostle James put it this way, "Knowing this, that the trying of your faith worketh patience. But let patience have her perfect work, that ye may be perfect and entire, wanting nothing," (James 1:3-4).

A Life Lesson:

My husband Steve knew there were changes going on within his company. But the day we heard the news, it was still difficult to swallow. Steve no longer had a job. The parent company had decided to reabsorb its satellite branch, and as a result his position had been eliminated. He was offered another job within the company, but it didn't line up with his qualifications. He felt it was time to move on.

With his experience and an impressive resume, I knew he'd be able to find another job. But the Lord's timing was different than mine.

A month into the job search, we received more devastating news. Our pastor, who had suffered with diabetes for years, had a heart attack and wasn't expected to make it. He passed away a few days later. My perspective was radically altered as I realized the magnitude of this loss versus the loss of Steve's job. I could be patient while Steve's job search continued.

With the death of our pastor, a pulpit committee was formed to begin the process of choosing a new minister. Steve was chosen to serve on the committee. He became one of three men enlisted with the task of prayerfully selecting our next pastor.

This was no small undertaking. And it required an investment of time – something Steve had because of the layoff. But I wasn't ready for the statement he made soon after the pulpit committee was formed. He didn't feel he'd be offered another job until the committee had identified the person who would take over as pastor. The process could take months, and Steve was okay with that.

I wish I could say I displayed a longsuffering attitude the entire time my husband was without a job. But I can't. I knew God would provide for us, but every time I witnessed our shrinking bank account, I was tempted to give in to fear. When would this trial end?

Nine months after Steve lost his job, the Lord provided him with employment. And you guessed it – our church had celebrated the arrival of our new pastor.

I learned a valuable lesson from a difficult trial: God is in control and He will provide. Choosing a longsuffering attitude would have given me a perspective that was pleasing to God.

Think about a time you chose to be longsuffering. How did it help you through your trial?_____

_____

_____

A Word from God's Word:

We're all familiar with the life of Job, but his response to suffering is worth a closer look. Job was described by God as an upright man who feared the Lord and avoided evil (Job 1:8). Satan wasn't impressed and issued a challenge: "…put forth thine hand now, and touch all that he hath, and he will curse thee to thy face," (Job 1:11).

God allowed Job to be severely tested. Over the course of twenty-four hours Job lost his wealth, the majority of his servants, and all of his children. Talk about total devastation. But notice the words that came from his mouth: "Naked came I out of my mother's womb, and naked shall I return thither: the Lord gave, and the Lord hath taken away; blessed be the name of the Lord. In all this Job sinned not, nor charged God foolishly." (Job 1:21-22)

Why do you think Job was able to maintain the right attitude in the face of such tragedy?_____

_____

Job realized that everything he had belonged to the Lord – the Lord had given it to him, and had chosen to take it all away. Job made the decision to worship the Lord regardless. But another trial was on its way.

Satan was given permission to afflict Job's body with painful boils. With good health a thing of the past, Job's wife suggested that he curse God and die.

How did Job respond? (Job 2:10)_____

_____

Job continued to choose the right attitude. He realized that life would include both good and bad. His trust in God triumphed over the bleakness of his circumstances.

We're not told how long Job suffered, but roughly thirty-five chapters are devoted to the conversation between Job and the three friends who came to comfort him. Instead of bringing solace to Job, however, each man only added to Job's misery by giving lengthy discourses as to why he was suffering. Discouragement set in, and Job cried out to God. Why was he allowed to go on living when he was in torment? God seemed so far away.

But God had a plan. When He spoke to Job, God described the greatness of His creation, and the awesomeness of His works. No direct answers to Job's questions were given, but no other explanation was needed. By the end of the conversation, Job repented for his limited view of God: "I know that thou canst do every thing, and that no thought can be withholden from thee," (Job 42:2).

Job was able to endure intense suffering because he chose to trust God. Even when he was at his lowest point, he still cried out to God instead of turning from Him.

How did the Lord respond to Job? (Job 42:10)_____

_____

The Lord accepted Job and gave him twice as much as he had before. Look at how the story ends: "So the Lord blessed the latter end of Job more than his beginning..." (Job 42:12a) What a beautiful picture of God's grace and goodness!

A Time to Reflect:

How would you describe your attitude when you're going through difficult trials? How does God want you to respond today?_____

_____

_____

Prayer: Heavenly Father, thank You for the real-life examples You give me in Your Word. Forgive me when I choose a bad attitude toward difficulties. Help me to remember You are in control, and You use trials to strengthen my faith and make me more like You. In Jesus' name, Amen.

Day 5

Years of Patience

A Moment to Meditate & Memorize:

Finish memorizing the verse for this week:

Psalm 86:15 But thou, O Lord, art a God full of compassion, and gracious, longsuffering, and plenteous in mercy and truth.

Think about the nature of God. Aren't you glad He's longsuffering? I'm thankful He pursued me when I was lost, and that He continues to extend grace when I sin. Consider the psalmist David's description of God: compassionate, gracious, longsuffering, and full of mercy and truth (Psalm 86:15).

A Life Lesson:

Home schooling can be challenging. Before our daughter Riley was born, Steve and I had made the decision to give it a try. I have to admit I was nervous. There was a lot at stake. If I failed, I could imagine Riley being unable to read or write – permanently scarred for life.

Maybe I was being overly cautious; but I chose a curriculum that offered everything in one kit so I would feel more confident. Teaching K-4 wasn't too bad; but just to be sure I was doing everything right I opted to use videos for K-5.

I wasn't the creative type. I depended on the daily lesson plans to lay out what Riley needed to complete each day, and I stuck to all of their recommendations. Home schooling was extremely structured and became an exercise in following the teacher's guide and making sure we finished everything on time.

As Riley moved from one grade to the next, I found myself emphasizing good grades more than a love for learning. I would get irritated with Riley when she didn't understand a concept the first time it was taught. My patience was wearing thin. The difficult truth was that I didn't want Riley to fail because I felt it would be a poor reflection on me.

We made the decision to enroll Riley in a Christian school when she began fourth grade. As an only child, we knew she would benefit from the interaction with her peers. Riley adjusted quickly to the transition – I was the one who had a hard time. I found myself still trying to manage Riley's performance.

It was so important to me that she get good grades, it became a daily routine to review how she had done on each test and quiz. When the occasional low grade showed up in the mix, my patience was nowhere to be found. I was the one who needed to learn a few things.

Thankfully God's response to our mistakes is different. I've messed up more times than I can count; yet God is longsuffering with me.

His Word accurately describes His love: "For he knoweth our frame; he remembereth that we are dust…But the mercy of the Lord is from everlasting to everlasting upon them that fear him, and his righteousness unto children's children," (Psalm 103:14,17). What a beautiful picture of His longsuffering nature.

How has God demonstrated His longsuffering nature to you?_____

_____

_____

A Word from God's Word:

Today's news can get pretty discouraging. A day doesn't go by without crime or violence making the headlines.

The same was true in Noah's day; in fact, it was much worse. God saw everything that was happening: "And God saw that the wickedness of man was great in the earth, and that every imagination of the thoughts of his heart was only evil continually," (Genesis 6:5).

Man's sin grieved the Lord so much that He regretted creating mankind. What did God plan to do? (Genesis 6:7)_____

_____

He would send a flood to destroy His creation – both man and animals. Before you start thinking this judgment was too harsh, consider the facts:

*God was willing to spare those who trusted in Him. (Genesis 6:8,14)

*God was longsuffering.

How many years did He give the people to repent? (Genesis 6:3) _____

_____

Yes, you read that correctly! I don't know about you, but I think 120 years is a mighty long time to put up with man's wickedness. God's longsuffering nature is seen over and over in His Word. The apostle Peter explains the reason behind this characteristic: "The Lord is not slack concerning his promise, as some men count slackness; but is longsuffering to us-ward, not willing that any should perish, but that all should come to repentance," (2 Peter 3:9).

In spite of the hideousness of man's sin, God wanted to give him every opportunity to repent – 120 years to repent. You can't get more longsuffering than that.

Building a massive boat in the dessert had to be quite a spectacle. Since it had never rained before, I'm sure Noah's construction project got more than a little attention. With a ready-made audience, Noah had plenty of opportunities to preach to the people about their sin and God's upcoming judgment. Would they listen?

After 120 long years, the ark was finished. Soon after Noah was done, big, wet drops began to fall from the sky. The people, who had mocked Noah and laughed at him, probably looked up with concern. As the rain continued, I can only imagine how many men, women, and children raced to the big boat, hoping there was still time to get on board. But God had already closed the door (Genesis 7:16).

How many people were spared from the devastation of the flood? (Genesis 7:13)_____

_____

Only 8 people chose to enter the ark: Noah and his wife, Shem, Ham, and Japheth, and their wives. In His omniscience, God had known all along that only Noah and his family would believe Him, yet in His patience God gave man plenty of time to turn to Him.

After the flood, the Lord said, "21...I will not again curse the ground any more for man's sake; for the imagination of man's heart is evil from his youth; neither will I again smite any more every thing living, as I have done. 22 While the earth remaineth, seedtime and harvest, and cold and heat, and summer and winter, and day and night shall not cease," (Genesis 8:21-22).

God's longsuffering nature is still evident today. He gives believers the privilege to share his truth with people everywhere, "But as we were allowed of God to be put in trust with the gospel, even so we speak; not as pleasing men, but God, which trieth our hearts," (1 Thessalonians 2:4).

A Time to Reflect:

Will you carry God's truth to others and choose to be longsuffering in the process? How does the Lord want you to respond today?_____

_____

_____

Prayer: Heavenly Father, thank You for the constant reminders of Your longsuffering nature. Forgive me when I get impatient. Help me yield to the Spirit in this area so I can accurately reflect You. In Jesus' name, Amen.

Questions for Group Discussion:

1. How did Joseph demonstrate a longsuffering attitude when he was put in prison for a crime he didn't commit?

2. How do you respond to others when they reject the truth you share from God's Word? What would have to change in order for your response to be like the apostle Paul's?

3. The book of Hosea details God's love for the nation of Israel. Describe how He treated Israel when the nation repeatedly strayed.

4. The Lord allowed Job to be severely tested. He lost his children, wealth, and physical health. What did Job say to his wife when she encouraged him to curse God and die? (Job 2:9).

5. According to the account of the flood in Genesis, is God longsuffering or not? Support your answer.

Week 5

Journey to Gentleness

Gentleness is thought of in terms of kind and mild treatment of others. When people are kind, it's fairly easy to respond with gentleness. But when inconvenienced or treated rudely, how should we respond? Each lesson in this chapter will challenge us to rely on the power of the Holy Spirit to respond the right way regardless of the scenario.

This week at a glance:

Day 1 – *Control that Tongue*

Day 2 – *Empty Promises*

Day 3 – *Avoiding Disaster*

Day 4 – *An Inconvenience or an Opportunity?*

Day 5 – *A Word Fitly Spoken*

Day 1

Control that Tongue

A Moment to Meditate & Memorize:

The topic we'll be studying this week is gentleness. Read through the verse several times and begin committing it to memory.

James 3:17 But the wisdom that is from above is first pure, then peaceable, gentle, and easy to be intreated, full of mercy and good fruits, without partiality, and without hypocrisy.

The power of the tongue is unbelievable. It can tear down and it can build up. We're given a warning: "But the tongue can no man tame; it is an unruly evil, full of deadly poison. Therewith bless we God, even the Father; and therewith curse we men, which are made after the similitude of God. Out of the same mouth proceedeth blessing and cursing…" James 3:8-10a

With so much at stake, we need to yield control of this small member to the Lord so our words remain gentle even under pressure.

A Life Lesson:

The bill came in the mail as usual. I was familiar with the amount we paid each month for our utilities, so I was shocked by the figure that was staring back at me from our cable statement. Since we had been without our land line, internet, and cable for a few days following a severe thunderstorm, I expected the opposite effect: a lower bill.

A quick look at the receipt revealed a couple problems. We hadn't been credited for the days we were without service, and we had been charged for a 12-month service protection plan we hadn't purchased. I was pretty irritated.

It was probably a good thing I didn't have time to take care of it immediately. I think I would have accused the unsuspecting service person of purposely overcharging us. My words would have been anything but gentle.

Fortunately, some time passed before I called the company. Instead of reacting emotionally to the mix-up, I was able to stick to the facts. The service person was extremely helpful – apologizing for the mistakes and promptly crediting our account for the days we were without service and for the protection plan we hadn't wanted.

I learned a valuable lesson: A gentle response when faced with an irritating situation accomplishes far more than responding in anger.

The book of Proverbs says it best: "A soft answer turneth away wrath: but grievous words stir up anger," (Proverbs 15:1). Allow the Holy Spirit to work in your life. His power can help you exchange harsh words for those that are gentle.

How do you respond when a person or situation irritates you?_____

A Word from God's Word:

I love seeing someone stand up for the underdog. Don't you? There's just something about one person encouraging another who isn't expected to do well, that stirs the heart of compassion in me. You probably feel the same way.

John Mark (Mark), a disciple in the New Testament, fits the bill of an underdog. He had gone on a missionary journey with the apostle Paul, and Barnabas. For some unknown reason he decided to return home prematurely.

He may have been discouraged by the persecution they had faced on their trip, or maybe he just missed his hometown. Whatever the reason, Mark's decision to leave rubbed Paul the wrong way. As a result, Paul lost all respect for this young man.

Time passed and Paul and Barnabas were planning a return visit to the believers in the towns they had initially visited. They wanted to check in with their brothers and sisters in Christ and help them continue to grow in the Lord. There was only one problem. Barnabas had chosen to bring a travelling companion with them whom Paul had rejected.

Who did Barnabas want to accompany them on their journey? (Acts 15:37)_

_____

Paul was adamant that John Mark should not come with them. He was shocked that Barnabas would suggest such a thing when Mark had left them in the middle of their previous mission trip. In Paul's mind, Mark was not reliable and wasn't fit for the ministry. A huge argument followed.

What ended up happening? (Acts 15:39)_____

_____

_____

Barnabas stood up for Mark and was willing to give him a second chance. Paul and Barnabas ended up going their separate ways: Paul took Silas and travelled to the churches in Syria and Cilicia, while Barnabas partnered with Mark and sailed to the churches in Cyprus.

Barnabas was convinced that God could still use John Mark. Although Mark made some poor decisions early on, by choosing to treat him with gentleness instead of harshness, Barnabas was able to restore him to an active role in the ministry.

Barnabas did the right thing. Years later, even Paul agreed.

What does Paul say about John Mark in 2 Timothy 4:11?_____

_____

_____

Treating others with gentleness in spite of their failures is an unmistakable fruit of the Spirit.

A Time to Reflect:

Who do you need to respond to with gentleness today?_____

_____

_____

Prayer: *Gracious Heavenly Father, thank You for dealing with me in gentleness rather than in anger. Help me to remember that a soft answer turns away wrath. I want to treat others with the same gentleness You show me. In Jesus' name, Amen.*

Day 2

Memory Problems

A Moment to Meditate & Memorize:

Continue committing this week's verse to memory.

James 3:17 But the wisdom that is from above is first pure, then peaceable, gentle, and easy to be intreated, full of mercy and good fruits, without partiality, and without hypocrisy.

We don't sign up for hardships, yet all of us experience them. When difficulties come calling we get to choose how to respond: with gentleness or bitterness.

The trial can either help us grow closer to the Lord, or cause us to turn away from Him. Jesus gave us the perfect example, "Who when he was reviled, reviled not again; when he suffered, he threatened not; but committed himself to him that judgeth righteously:" (1 Peter 2:23)

A Life Lesson:

We all mess up, but I'm inspired when others go through adversity and maintain the right attitude in spite of it. I'm grateful for my friend, *Heidi, who showed me what it looks like to trust in the Lord and continue demonstrating love to a family that rejects her.

Heidi has a difficult life: her husband makes the majority of the income, yet refuses to give her money for groceries and necessities. Her son has health issues and battles a drug addiction. And her daughter is intent on building her own life.

No one can deny this is a tough situation, one that could leave the strongest person defeated. But Heidi chooses to cling to hope. When her husband treats her with disrespect, she responds with gentleness. How does she do it?

She knows the real problem is that her family members don't know the Lord. Heidi realizes she's the only Christian witness in their lives, and she desperately wants them to accept the Savior she loves.

She meets weekly with ladies from her church to pray. She lives out her faith in front of her family, just like the apostle Peter instructed: "1 Likewise, ye wives, be in subjection to your own husbands; that, if any obey not the word, they also may without the word be won by the conversation of the wives; 2 While they behold your chaste conversation coupled with fear," (1 Peter 3:1-2).

Instead of walking away from a seemingly impossible situation, Heidi is determined to stay and be the example of Christ in her home.

*name changed for protection

How have you seen gentleness modeled in the life of a Christian friend?_____

_____

_____

A Word from God's Word:

Jesus often illustrated heavenly truths using parables. Remember the story of the unforgiving servant? Jesus contrasted gentle forgiveness with harsh blame.

The servant's debt was enormous: ten thousand talents to be exact. He had borrowed money from the king and now it was time to settle his account. I imagine his hands grew clammy as he thought about having to face the king with his confession.

He didn't have the means to pay back the loan. Ten thousand talents would be well over a hundred billion dollars in today's economy. Even if his salary was multiplied many times over and he worked for the rest of his life, he would be unable to pay back everything he owed. How would the king respond?

He didn't have to wait long to find out. What was the king's command? (Matthew 18:25)_____

_____

_____

The servant, his wife, children, and all that he had were to be sold. What heartbreaking words to hear.

Immediately the servant fell to his knees begging for mercy: "Lord, have patience with me, and I will pay thee all," (Matthew 18:26). I'm not sure what he expected, but his words went straight to the king's heart. Something changed.

What did the lord of the servant do? (Matthew 18:27)_____

_____

_____

He was filled with compassion toward the servant, forgave him the debt he owed, and let him go. The king treated the servant with gentleness when he didn't deserve it. What relief the servant must have felt! But his gratefulness was short-lived.

The servant went in search of a man who owed him an hundred pence – the equivalent of about four months wages. He grabbed him by the throat and demanded his money.

The man fell down at the servant's feet begging for mercy. He promised to pay everything he owed, if only the servant would be patient with him. The words should have jogged the servant's memory. If they did, he ignored them.

What was the servant's response? (Matthew 18:30)_____

_____

_____

He refused to forgive the man. Instead he had the man put in prison until he could pay off his debt.

Forgiveness is proof of a gentle spirit – one that is controlled by the Lord Jesus Christ.

A Time to Reflect:

Do you hold grudges? What step will you take today to replace a harsh spirit with one that is gentle?_____

_____

_____

Prayer: Gracious Heavenly Father, thank You for forgiving me of an enormous sin debt. Forgive me for holding grudges and treating others harshly, when You've pardoned so much. Help me submit to the work of the Holy Spirit so I can respond to others with a gentle spirit. In Jesus' name, Amen.

Day 3

Avoiding Disaster

A Moment to Meditate & Memorize:

Continue memorizing the verse for this week.

James 3:17 But the wisdom that is from above is first pure, then peaceable, gentle, and easy to be intreated, full of mercy and good fruits, without partiality, and without hypocrisy.

Taking responsibility for our actions can be tough when we mess up. But taking responsibility for someone else's mistake is almost unheard of. Let the Lord speak to your heart today as we continue to study the quality of gentleness.

A Life Lesson:

It seemed like a good deal. Workers came through our neighborhood offering to spread pine straw for less than my husband, Steve, and I would pay for the pine straw alone. Our yard would look a lot better and we wouldn't have to invest countless hours spreading the straw ourselves.

The only thing we would still need to do was excavate our pond. The workers assured us they could tackle that project over the next couple of days as well. The decision seemed simple – we'd be foolish to pass up their offer.

They began spreading the pine straw immediately. Two hours later the job was finished. We were handed an enormous bill, and we realized our mistake. We hadn't counted how many bales of pine straw the workers actually used. With a large yard, and no way to prove them wrong, we ended up paying the exorbitant amount.

We were pretty sure the workers had taken advantage of us. When they showed up to remove the sand from our pond, Steve questioned them about the initial bill. They guaranteed us they had spread 300 bales of pine straw in the two-hour time period. We weren't convinced.

As the day went by, I became increasingly uncomfortable with the quality of their work. Steve had to remind them several times to remove the debris from the pond, instead of moving it from one side of the pond to the other. I could hear raised voices as I attempted to go about my business.

When Steve came inside, I could tell by the disgusted look on his face that the conversation had not gone well. He wanted me to come out and verify the initial terms we had agreed upon. They had conveniently forgotten the details. No doubt about it, the job was hard work. But they had given their word that they would complete it.

It was difficult to control my anger. I felt we had been cheated. Their lies didn't sit well with me, and I found it difficult to stick with the facts. My words weren't kind and they were anything but gentle.

I was shaking when I returned to the house. Although the workers were wrong, I hadn't exactly been walking in the Spirit when I responded to them. Instead of seeing a glimpse of the Savior, they had seen my old nature. I had to apologize.

It's easy to take offense when we've been wronged. That's what people expect. When we submit to the power of the Holy Spirit and gentleness replaces anger, others take notice and are drawn to the Lord.

Write about a time when you responded with gentleness. What was the result?_____

_____

_____

A Word from God's Word:

David couldn't believe his ears. He and his men had protected Nabal's shepherds and flocks while they were in Carmel. Now Nabal was refusing to return the kindness with food and provisions for David and his men. Nabal was certainly living up to the meaning of his name: fool.

What was Nabal's response to the messengers David sent? (1 Samuel 25:10-11) _____

_____

Apparently Nabal wasn't moved by the kindness shown by David, nor did he respond with gentleness. In a characteristic display of bad manners, Nabal let David's messengers know they weren't getting any help from him. He questioned their motives and treated them rudely.

When David got the news, his first thought was retaliation. No one was going to treat him and his men with such disrespect. He let his anger bubble to the surface and issued the command: "Gird ye on every man his sword," (1 Samuel 25:13a). An army of four hundred men followed David back to Carmel.

One of Nabal's servants had overheard the conversation between his master and David's men. He went to warn Nabal's wife, Abigail. Surely David would be highly offended when he found out about Nabal's refusal to help him and would come back seeking revenge.

What did Abigail do? (1 Samuel 25:18-20) _____

_____

After preparing a huge meal for David and his men, Abigail saddled her donkey and set off – no doubt giving careful thought as to what she would say when she met the approaching army. She didn't have to wait long.

David must have been shocked to see a woman on a donkey riding toward him. Only moments before he was planning his attack; now curiosity got the best of him. Was she an enemy?

When she was just a short distance away, she dismounted and bowed before David with her face to the ground. David discovered this was Nabal's wife, Abigail. Her words and actions stood in stark contrast to those of her husband. He had reacted with suspicion and harshness, but Abigail's words were honest and gentle. She willingly took the blame for her husband's poor behavior; yet tried to make up for them by meeting David's original request for food and provisions.

Instead of hiding from the situation her husband caused, Abigail willingly took the blame for her husband's poor behavior. She met David's original request by providing food for him and his men. Abigail's gentle words and actions caused David to change his plans.

What was David's original plan before speaking to Abigail? (1 Samuel 25:34)_____

_____

David and his men would have killed Nabal, his family, and all of his men. Instead, Abigail's gentle spirit diffused David's anger, he accepted her apology, and he and his men returned to their camp.

Responding to anger with words of gentleness is proof of the Holy Spirit's fruit in a person's life. Give Him control today.

A Time to Reflect:

How does the Lord want you to respond to the lesson today?_____

_____

_____

Prayer: Heavenly Father, thank You for this illustration of gentleness in action. It's easy to get upset when others are angry with me. Help me to be keenly aware of the Holy Spirit in my life so I can submit my words to His authority before I speak. Let my words be truthful and gentle. In Jesus' name, Amen.

Day 4

An Inconvenience or an Opportunity?

A Moment to Meditate & Memorize:

Continue memorizing the verse for this week.

James 3:17 But the wisdom that is from above is first pure, then peaceable, gentle, and easy to be intreated, full of mercy and good fruits, without partiality, and without hypocrisy.

How do you respond when your plans are interrupted? If you're like me, it can be challenging to choose a gracious attitude.

As we submit more and more to God's work in our lives, we'll be able to welcome these interruptions as opportunities rather than inconveniences.

A Life Lesson:

I've lost track of the many times my friend Patricia has come to my rescue. But one instance stands out in my mind. Our daughter Riley was graduating from high school and we were planning a big party. I knew we'd need to pick a color scheme and plan a menu, but I really didn't know where to begin.

Patricia is the multi-talented, artistic type. A couple months before graduation she asked me what I had planned for Riley's party. I don't remember what I said. I just remember by the end of the conversation, Patricia had offered to help out with all of the details.

I was stunned and thrilled at the same time. Patricia is one of those ladies who are involved in a thousand things – raising her family, teaching Bible studies, working on several committees at church, and the list goes on.

I knew her party-planning skills were phenomenal, but I didn't want to add another thing to her to-do list. She would have to take time out of her busy schedule to sit down with Riley and me to discuss what we had in mind; and then spend additional time working up a menu and décor for the celebration.

Instead of viewing the task as an inconvenience, Patricia's gentle response assured me she was genuinely excited to help out. As we planned the party and implemented each step, I saw the fruit of the Spirit demonstrated in her life.

She was willing to take time out of her already-busy schedule to help us shop for just the right decorations. What we were unable to find at the store, she let us borrow from her personal collection. She walked us through every detail from the amount of food we would need per person to how we should arrange the guest tables on our deck for maximum seating capacity. As the day of the party approached, she even sent me text messages letting me know she was praying for dry weather when the forecast called for rain.

What Patricia could have viewed as an inconvenience, she embraced as an opportunity. Her gentle response to help me in spite of her other commitments, taught me the importance of a life yielded to the Holy Spirit.

Is there a situation you're facing that requires a gentle response? How will you respond?_____

_____

_____

A Word from God's Word:

There was a lot to do. Rebekah carried her empty pitcher to the well, focused on finishing her evening chores. Once the pitcher was filled, she carefully placed it on her shoulder. Her thoughts were interrupted when a man ran up to her and asked for a drink of water.

She hadn't seen the stranger before, but that didn't matter. Rebekah knew what she needed to do. The man must be tired after a long day's journey. She noticed several dusty camels kneeling a few feet away. She immediately gave the man a drink from her pitcher.

Although she had been interrupted, Rebekah didn't give a second thought to being inconvenienced.

What did she offer to do in addition to giving the stranger a drink? (Genesis 24:19)_____

_____

Rebekah gave water to the man's ten camels. It's easy to imagine the camels were thirsty after travelling a good distance. Each camel could drink 30-50 gallons of water apiece. Drawing that much water for so many camels would take a considerable amount of time. Rebekah's gentle spirit enabled her to willingly serve this man and his camels.

The story doesn't end there. It was no coincidence that this stranger was the servant of Rebekah's uncle Abraham. He had come to Mesopotamia for a specific reason.

Why had Abraham sent his servant to the city where his brother Nahor lived? (Genesis 24:4)_____

_____

Abraham commissioned his servant to go to Mesopotamia to find a wife for Isaac. The servant had prayed for specific guidance on his quest. He asked the Lord to send a woman to the well that would be willing to give him a drink and would also offer to give his camels water. God answered his prayer by sending Rebekah.

Arranged marriages were the custom of the day. Rebekah's father Bethuel was in favor of allowing her to marry Isaac. Abraham's servant was overjoyed and worshipped the Lord.

Eager to return to Abraham, the servant prepared to leave the next day. But Rebekah's mother and brother weren't quite ready to let Rebekah go. They wanted her to remain for at least ten days (Genesis 24:55). Ultimately, they left the decision up to Rebekah.

What was Rebekah's response? (Genesis 24:58)_____

_____

Over the course of 24 hours Rebekah's life had altered dramatically. Who would have thought a gentle response to a stranger would result in marriage to her uncle Abraham's son, Isaac? Instead of questioning God's will for her life, Rebekah trusted the plan He had for her and chose to act on the next step that was before her – she would leave with Abraham's servant immediately to become Isaac's wife.

When faced with inconvenience, a gentle answer accompanied by action is sure to point others to the Savior.

A Time to Reflect:

List some ways you can prepare yourself to give a gentle response to those who inconvenience you today:_____

_____

_____

Prayer: Heavenly Father, thank You for the circumstances You allow in my life. I know You are at work, conforming me to the image of Your Son. Forgive me for focusing too much on myself. Help me recognize "inconveniences" as Your divine interruptions. Help me respond with a gentle spirit. In Jesus' name, Amen.

Day 5

A Word Fitly Spoken

A Moment to Meditate & Memorize:

Finish memorizing this week's verse.

James 3:17 But the wisdom that is from above is first pure, then peaceable, gentle, and easy to be intreated, full of mercy and good fruits, without partiality, and without hypocrisy.

We will never understand all there is to know about our Savior, until we reach heaven one day. Isaiah clarified, "For my thoughts are not your thoughts, neither are your ways my ways saith the Lord," (Isaiah 55:8). But we do have his Word – rich with character qualities to emulate, like gentleness.

A Life Lesson:

The dog's incessant whining continued throughout the day. Although Steve and I didn't pay much attention to it at first, by the time the second day rolled around, we were beginning to get tired of the obnoxious sound.

Why was the dog making so much noise? We had never heard the dog put up such a fuss. Maybe it was a new puppy and wasn't used to being away from its mother. Or maybe it didn't like being left outside for so long.

We could see the dachshund in our neighbor's backyard. It didn't look like anything was wrong. There were bowls on the back porch leading us to believe the little dog had plenty of food and water. But the whining continued.

I was none too happy when the dog's mournful cry woke me in the middle of the night. Why wasn't the neighbor trying to quiet her dog? I grew more frustrated as the minutes ticked by.

Apparently, we weren't the only ones being serenaded by the noisy dog. Our neighbors up the street began complaining about the backyard bawler. Something had to be done.

My husband was concerned. Maybe the dog was sick, or needed more food and water. I wasn't so compassionate. I just wanted a reprieve from the noise. Steve hopped the fence to try and figure out what was going on. When no one responded to his knock on the back door, he got the neighbor's telephone number off the dog's collar.

Steve called its owner. Although no one answered, he was able to leave a message. He let the owner know he was concerned about her pet, had gone over to check on the dog, and was wondering if there was anything he could do.

A few days later we got a thank you card in the mail. I didn't recognize the return address as I slit open the envelope. It was from our neighbor with the dachshund. She wrote to thank us for being concerned about her dog. She had been called away on a family emergency and had to leave the dog behind. Although her son was stopping by to feed the dog, it was extremely lonely. She apologized profusely for the dog's whining and thanked us for being thoughtful enough to call her.

I handed the card to my husband, knowing that I didn't deserve the words. I had only cared about how the dog's whining was affecting me. Steve was the one who had demonstrated a gentle spirit – checking on the dog, and contacting the owner to see if he could help.

God can use any situation to teach powerful truth. The Holy Spirit can make it possible for us to cultivate the fruit of gentleness. Be ready.

A Word from God's Word:

The miracles of Jesus were incredible: the lame could walk, the deaf could hear, and those with leprosy were made whole. No wonder crowds gathered wherever He went. But physical healing was not the only reason people sought Jesus.

Why did parents bring their children to Jesus in Matthew 19:13?_____

_____

These parents simply wanted Jesus to touch their children and pray for them. It seems they understood the importance of dedicating their sons and daughters to the Lord. But not everyone thought this was a wise use of Jesus' time.

Used to seeing Jesus debate with religious leaders and teach grown-ups spiritual truths, the disciples decided they needed to protect Jesus' schedule. Maybe they planned on going to another town that day, or maybe they were just tired. Whatever their reasoning, they had run out of patience.

How did the disciples respond to the parents who brought their children to Jesus? (Mark 10:13)_____

_____

A stern rebuke is never easy to handle. The disciples' disapproval and criticism could be heard in the tone of their voices. I can only imagine the parents' responses. Some of them may have felt guilty for interrupting Jesus and were ready to leave with their children in tow. Others might have stared in surprise.

But Jesus was not pleased with the disciples' outburst. Jesus' gentle response validated the parents' mission.

What did Jesus say in response to the disciples' rebuke? (Mark 10:14)_____

_____

_____

It seems the disciples still had a lot to learn from their Master. Jesus was never too busy to spend time with those who sought Him. He knew these children and their parents trusted Him. Their faith would be rewarded.

What did Jesus do? (Mark 10:16)_____

_____

In stark contrast to the disciples' reprimand, Jesus blessed the children who came to Him. Jesus' words of acceptance and caring touch encouraged the children to draw near to Him. Each one was rewarded with Jesus' blessing.

When others are in need of help, a choice has to be made – respond selfishly or selflessly. By demonstrating a gentle, selfless spirit, people will come face to face with the fruit of the Spirit.

A Time to Reflect:

How does the Lord want you to respond to the lesson today?_____

_____

_____

_____

Prayer: Heavenly Father, thank You for reminding me of what is important to You. Forgive me when I act selfishly to meet my own needs, ignoring the needs of others. Help me to choose a servant-attitude and allow Your Spirit to grow the fruit of gentleness in my life today. In Jesus' name, Amen.

Questions for Group Discussion:

1. What happened as a result of Barnabas treating John Mark with gentleness? (Acts 15:36-39)

2. God has forgiven you of a sin debt you could never repay. How do you treat others who sin against you?

3. What caused David to change his mind about killing Nabal, his family, and servants? (1 Samuel 25:32-34)

4. How would Rebekah's life have been different had she chosen to go about her business and deny the request of Abraham's servant?

5. Jesus is ready and eager to meet with each one of us. What challenged you most this week? Write a prayer to the Lord about it.

Week 6

The Battle Between Good & Evil

God is the ultimate example of all that is good. His definition of love admonishes us to reject evil thinking and avoid rejoicing when we hear something bad about others. He encourages us to follow in His footsteps, demonstrating His goodness to those around us. The five lessons in this chapter will encourage us to choose good over evil.

This week at a glance:

Day 1 – *No Comparison*

Day 2 – *Beware of Greed*

Day 3 – *Temptation's Lure*

Day 4 – *Works that Reflect*

Day 5 – *More Than We Deserve*

Day 1

No Comparison

A Moment to Meditate & Memorize:

This week's topic is goodness. Read through the verse several times and begin committing it to memory.

Psalm 107:8 Oh that men would praise the Lord for his goodness, and for his wonderful works to the children of men!

Entitlement is a big problem in today's society. Because God is good, we expect certain things and don't appreciate them for the blessings they are. I have to admit, I'm guilty.

Today we'll take a look at the mistake of comparing ourselves with others, and we'll be challenged to focus on the One who deserves our attention and praise for His goodness toward us.

A Life Lesson:

Have you ever played the comparison game? Sometimes I don't even realize I'm playing until I notice how discontent I've become.

Writing can be a difficult career. There are times when the words just won't come. I can be distracted by social media and the need to get my work in front of more readers. The pressure to produce an article from a fresh perspective can be intense. Some days, I just don't feel like writing.

Other writers I know don't seem to be struggling. Their pieces are witty and widely-read. A slew of comments points to the fact that their audience is engaged with their writing. Instead of being thankful for the handful of comments on my site, I wonder why there aren't more. In all honesty, there are days when I feel like my writing doesn't make a difference. It's difficult to continue.

The comparison game only makes me miserable. God's Word reminds me: "For we dare not make ourselves of the number, or compare ourselves with some that commend themselves: but they measuring themselves by themselves, and comparing themselves among themselves, are not wise," (2 Corinthians 10:12). It causes me to negate the blessings of God, and shift my focus to things other than Him.

I'm quick to forget the goodness of God. He has given me the opportunity to make writing a career – I don't have to work a full-time job and relegate writing to my free time. He's allowed me to grow in my craft and experience support through a writer's group and on-line classes. He's even made it possible for me to connect and develop friendships with other believers across the world.

I take so many things for granted: the beauty of God's creation, health, freedom, the opportunity to worship. Instead of seeing these things for what they are – a demonstration of God's goodness, I view them as rights and fail to praise Him for them.

I've often resembled the children of Israel who were freed from slavery, but began murmuring and grumbling shortly after their sandals left Egyptian soil. Although I've never experienced bondage like they did, I tend to hitch a ride on the same wagon of complaints they often rode.

God's ultimate purpose is for me to be conformed to the image of His Son (Romans 8:29). Instead of comparisons and complaints, God desires my worship and praise. His Word shows me what I need to put into practice: "Praise ye the Lord. Praise God in his sanctuary: praise him in the firmament of his power. Praise him for his mighty acts: praise him according to his excellent greatness," (Psalm 150:1-2). God is good.

How will you praise the Lord for His goodness today?_____

_____

_____

A Word from God's Word:

God's goodness is easy to see: He gives us every new day, provides us with food to eat and clothes to wear, gives us family and friends, and comforts us when we're down. This character quality is part of God's nature.

The Bible is full of examples of the goodness of God. He extends salvation to everyone.

Write Acts 2:21 in the space provided:_____

_____

_____

We don't deserve salvation, yet God willingly sent His Son to die on the cross, to pay our sin debt, so we could be reconciled to Him. The ultimate display of goodness. Even when we sin, God doesn't abandon us.

In Psalm 107, David recounted the stories of people experiencing a wide range of difficulties. In each circumstance God demonstrated His goodness, which caused the psalmist to reiterate words worth remembering: "Oh that men would praise the Lord for his goodness, and for his wonderful works to the children of men!" (Psalm 107:8,15,21,31).

The children of Israel got to experience God's goodness firsthand. They had been in exile in the land of Babylon for 70 years. Now they were free! Cyrus the Great ended the Babylonian captivity of the Jews. They could return to Judah. It would take several weeks to make the 900 mile trek, but they would be home.

The barren wilderness between Babylon and Judah proved to be more than they could handle. They ran out of supplies and became faint and discouraged. The desperation of their situation caused them to cry out to God.

How did God respond? (Psalm 107:6-7)_____

_____

In His grace, He answered and delivered them, and led them out of their distress. The Israelites were grateful, but their gratitude didn't last long. Once the trial was past, they soon forgot God's goodness until they bumped into another difficulty. Does this sound familiar?

The psalmist addressed what happened when people had health problems. Sickness reminded them just how frail they were. They realized they were not in control – so they called out to God.

What was God's response? (Psalm 107:19-20)_____

_____

He healed them. What a good God!

No matter what trial we face, God is always good. His long track record proves it. Praise God for His goodness and allow the Holy Spirit to develop this fruit in you.

A Time to Reflect:

How does the Lord want you to respond to the lesson?_____

_____

_____

_____

Prayer: *Heavenly Father, thank You for being so good. Forgive me when I take Your blessings for granted and forget to praise You for them. Help me praise You openly for who You are and all You've done. Help me yield to the Spirit so others will see Your goodness in me, and be drawn to You. In Jesus' name, Amen.*

Day 2

Beware of Greed

A Moment to Meditate & Memorize:

Continue committing this week's verse to memory:

Psalm 107:8 Oh that men would praise the Lord for his goodness, and for his wonderful works to the children of men!

Have your motives ever been less than pure? The process of reasoning and planning begins with thoughts. Today's lesson will provide examples to help you make the right choice between good and evil.

A Life Lesson:

We knew the church was struggling financially. Offerings during the summer months were considerably lower than normal. The situation didn't look good. Would enough money come in to continue paying all the bills?

Where we saw an obstacle, God saw an opportunity. After mowing the grass one evening, my husband Steve came into the house with some challenging news. He had been praying about the church finances and knew God could meet the need.

He was willing to substantially increase our giving if the Lord provided the necessary income. I was shocked. Although I was excited to see my husband take this step of faith, I wanted him to be reasonable. His proposal seemed like a wild stretch to me, and I wasn't totally on board; but I couldn't help exploring the possibilities.

My thoughts shifted from Steve's generosity to what we would do with any extra money he earned. Greed shot to the surface; I did a good job of spending the money before it was ever a reality. Enough daydreaming. Time to face the facts.

The economy wasn't exactly booming. And Steve's software sales had been very slow up to that point. I had to be realistic - I was doubtful anything would happen.

Two months later, Steve's job changed from covering new accounts to selling products to existing customers. What began as a dismal year suddenly got exciting. As one deal after another closed, I saw evidence of God's hand at work and embraced the plan Steve had outlined in the summer.

By the end of December, Steve had exceeded his quota. God's provision and Steve's willingness to be part of the solution to meet our church's need, paved the way for us to witness the goodness of our Heavenly Father.

It was a privilege to follow through on the financial commitment we had made. Greed and doubt almost caused me to miss an opportunity to experience God's goodness. His grace allowed me to see it.

Write about a time when you experienced God's goodness in spite of a bad attitude:_____

_____

_____

A Word from God's Word:

He had witnessed the impossible; the captain of the Syrian army had been cured of leprosy. Being diagnosed with this dreaded disease was akin to a death sentence. There was no cure. But after washing seven times in the Jordan River as the prophet Elisha had instructed him, the captain stood before them with no trace of the disease.

Gehazi listened closely while his master, Elisha, talked to Naaman the Syrian. Naaman was presenting Elisha with gifts as a token of his appreciation for being healed. But Elisha wouldn't take what was offered.

What did Elisha say to Naaman? (2 Kings 5:16)_____

_____

Elisha refused the gift, and sent Naaman back home in peace.

Gehazi must have been stunned. His master had given Naaman a new lease on life. Surely that was worth something. He wouldn't mind having the gifts his master had rejected. It didn't take him long to come up with a plan.

He ran after Naaman and his entourage. The caravan slowed and Naaman stopped his chariot and voiced his concern. Gehazi assured him that everything was fine. Now was the time to put his plan into action.

What did Gehazi tell Naaman? (2 Kings 5:22)_____

_____

_____

The lie slipped smoothly from Gehazi's lips: two of the sons of the prophets had arrived at Elisha's door shortly after Naaman left. They were in need of some clothes and money. Would Naaman be willing to supply the need? Of course Naaman was more than happy to help.

Gehazi couldn't help patting himself on the back. His scheme had worked perfectly. He now had some new clothes and lots of money. And no one was the wiser – or so he thought.

When he returned to his master's house, Elisha asked where he'd been. Another lie came out of Gehazi's mouth as he assured Elisha that he hadn't gone anywhere.

The same God that healed Naaman's leprosy had revealed Gehazi's whereabouts to Elisha. Elisha confronted Gehazi. Naaman didn't even have to respond. The game was up.

Sin has consequences. Instead of being grateful that Naaman had the chance to experience the goodness of God, Gehazi focused on the opportunity to gain material wealth.

What happened to Gehazi? (2 Kings 5:27)_____

_____

He became a leper. And if that wasn't bad enough, Gehazi's descendents were also plagued with leprosy; an astronomical price to pay for a few clothes and some money.

The story of Gehazi provides a great picture of the temptations each of us face. When we are tempted, we can choose good thoughts or evil thoughts. Good thoughts will become good actions that lead to good consequences.

Make the decision to "Walk in the Spirit, and ye shall not fulfil the lust of the flesh," (Galatians 5:16). Goodness is a fruit of the Spirit at work in your life.

A Time to Reflect:

Let the Lord examine your thoughts. How does He want you to respond?___

_____

_____

_____

Prayer: Heavenly Father, thank You for giving me a clear example of good versus evil. Help me recognize evil thoughts that aren't consistent with Your will. When I stay focused on You and am submitted to Your plan, the Holy Spirit can develop the fruit of goodness in my life. In Jesus' name, Amen.

Day 3

Temptations' Lure

A Moment to Meditate & Memorize:

Continue working on this week's memory verse:

Psalm 107:8 Oh that men would praise the Lord for his goodness, and for his wonderful works to the children of men!

Every day we're bombarded with tempting thoughts. The choices we make will have either positive or negative consequences. In his grace, God can use our mistakes and those of others, to teach us valuable lessons.

Read today's entry and take it to heart. Let God's goodness inspire you to yield more fully to Him instead of leaning on your own understanding.

A Life Lesson:

The test was the next day. Instead of preparing ahead of time, I waited until the night before the test to study – not the wisest thing to do.

I remember reviewing the science material after dinner and talking to one of my friends on the phone for a while. It was getting late. I still had some studying to do and some conversions to memorize before I'd be done. That's when the tempting thought entered my mind.

The teacher was going to let us use a handout during the test. Instead of having to memorize the final pages of my notes, I could just write the information on the back of that paper. What a brilliant idea! It would save me hours of study time.

But wouldn't that be cheating? I dismissed the truth before I could give it much thought. I started transferring the conversions from my notes to the handout. Within minutes I was done.

Science class was my second subject the next day. I thought I was pretty clever as I headed to class with my handout. The information I hadn't memorized was neatly written on the back of the paper.

I was early. The minutes ticked by slowly, and I started getting nervous. Was the teacher looking at me strangely? Or was it just my over-active imagination? I asked him a question or two about the test material. My hands grew clammy. I tried to act normal.

As my teacher passed out the tests, he explained the directions. Because we were allowed to use our handouts, he would be checking to make sure nothing else was written on them.

I couldn't believe it. There was no time to erase any of the information on my handout. The science teacher was heading to my desk. He tapped my shoulder to let me know he was aware that I had tried to cheat.

I barely made it through the rest of the day. Guilt overwhelmed me. I felt physically ill. Acting on one temptation had left me with a boatload of trouble.

Sin always has consequences. Because I didn't make the right choice when temptation came calling, I failed my science test and disappointed both my parents and teacher.

It's important to evaluate our thoughts in the light of God's Word. Choosing his ways when we're tempted allows good to triumph over evil every time.

"There hath no temptation taken you but such as is common to man: but **God is faithful**, who will not suffer you to be tempted above that ye are able; but will with the temptation also make a way to escape, that ye may be able to bear it." (1 Corinthians 10:13; emphasis added)

What consequences have you experienced when you've made poor choices?_

_____

_____

A Word from God's Word:

Life is filled with temptations. We must choose between right and wrong – good and evil.

Lot's story was no different. We're introduced to him early in the book of Genesis. Lot was Abram's nephew. After the Lord told Abram to leave Ur, he began his journey. Because Lot's father had died, Lot went with his uncle, Abram.

No doubt, Lot had heard the story many times. The Lord had appeared to his uncle and told him to leave his country and everything he was familiar with and go to another land. He promised He would make a great nation out of Abram – blessing those who blessed him and cursing those who cursed him. (Genesis 12:1-3)

But the promise and its fulfillment were separated by many years. Both Abram and Lot had become wealthy men with lots of cattle - there wasn't enough land to support them both. The uncomfortable situation led to arguing and Abram proposed a solution.

What solution did Abram propose? (Genesis 13:9)_____

_____

_____

They should separate from each other. Abram gave Lot first choice of the land that lay before them. After looking it over carefully, Lot decided on the well-watered plain of Jordan. His cattle would have ample food and there were cities close by. There was only one problem.

What was wrong with the city of Sodom? (Genesis 13:13)_____

_____

The men of Sodom were wicked sinners. Instead of checking into things more closely, Lot made his decision based on what his eyes could see. The land itself was perfect for his cattle, but the people would have a devastating effect on his family.

Instead of staying on the outskirts of Sodom, Lot eventually moved his family into the city where he held a position of authority. His decisions had continued to go from bad to worse. The wickedness of Sodom and another city in close proximity, Gomorrah, were ripe for God's judgment. God promised Abram He would spare the cities if He found ten righteous people living there.

What happened? (Genesis 19:15-16)_____

_____

There weren't even ten righteous people. God would have to bring judgment on the city. God's angels urged Lot and his family to leave and yet they lingered. The Lord, in His mercy, brought them out.

Lot, his wife, and two daughters got out of the city before God rained fire and brimstone down on both Sodom and Gomorrah. God's instructions had been clear; they were to escape to the mountains and not look back. Unwilling to make a final break from her former life, Lot's wife turned back for one final glimpse of their city.

What did she turn into? (Genesis 19:26)_____

_____

She became a pillar of salt. What began as a seemingly innocent decision – to move to a nice piece of land close to some cities – became a tragedy in the life of Lot. Not only did he lose the valuable guidance of his uncle Abram, but he lost his testimony, and even lost his wife.

Continually choosing evil over good will yield dreadful consequences. Good decisions are possible with God's help. Allow the Holy Spirit to continue developing this fruit in your life today.

A Time to Reflect:

Do you struggle with making good decisions? How does the Lord want you to respond to the lesson today?_____

_____

_____

_____

Prayer: *Heavenly Father thank You for the warning from the life of Lot. When I look to You, good decisions are possible in the face of temptation. Help me consistently make right choices through the power of the Holy Spirit. Cultivate goodness in me today. In Jesus' name, Amen.*

Day 4

Works that Reflect

A Moment to Meditate & Memorize:

Continue working on this week's memory verse:

Psalm 107:8 Oh that men would praise the Lord for his goodness, and for his wonderful works to the children of men!

How do you spend your time? Do you choose activities that only benefit you, or do they also help others? Read today's lesson and consider the "good works" the Lord has called you to do. (Ephesians 2:10).

A Life Lesson:

It was a new year. The demands on my friend's time were already pulling her in a million directions. Her husband and boys were a top priority.

She wanted to be intentional with her time. Her talents were as many and varied as the opportunities before her. It was difficult for to say "No." She felt the need to evaluate everything on her plate.

After spending time in prayer, she decided to narrow her focus. She wanted to concentrate on tasks that would have eternal significance. If the position would give her a chance to be the hands and feet of Christ and open doors for her to share the gospel, she would get involved.

In the middle of kingdom work, a crisis occurred. The news wasn't good. Her husband had suffered a stroke, and she had taken him to the emergency room.

I could only imagine all the fears and questions she must have faced in those first hours following her husband's stroke. In spite of whatever internal struggle she may have been experiencing, she cared for her husband and family and continued to be an encouragement to those who came by to visit.

Even while she was in need of support, she became familiar with the needs of the hospital staff, and offered to pray for them. The fruit of the Spirit was clearly visible.

Instead of becoming bitter at God for the difficult circumstances He had allowed in her life, she chose to cultivate the fruit of goodness.

How do you respond when a crisis occurs? What step will you take to allow the fruit of goodness to grow in your life?_____

_____

_____

A Word from God's Word:

The women were heart-broken. It was still hard to grasp the fact that their friend, Dorcas, (also known as Tabitha) was dead. She had been a faithful disciple. Her faith was evident in her actions – she was constantly doing things for others. She had a soft spot for the widows in her community.

Dorcas had gotten sick and instead of recovering, she had died. In their sorrow, her friends prepared her body for burial. Oh, how they would miss her. Wasn't there anything else they could do for her?

In the neighboring town of Lydda, the apostle Peter had healed a man who had been unable to move. Maybe word had made it to Joppa of this amazing miracle. Or perhaps they were unable to accept the death of their friend Dorcas. Whatever their reason, these female disciples were stirred by a sliver of hope. Could Peter help them?

What did the ladies do? (Acts 9:38)_____

_____

They sent two men to Lydda to find Peter and beg him to come to Joppa as soon as he could. Maybe he could do something.

By the time Peter arrived, widows and friends were mourning the loss of Dorcas. Tears coursed down their cheeks as they showed Peter the coats and clothing she had made for them.

Peter responded by sending everyone out of the room. He kneeled down and prayed.

What happened? (Acts 9:40)_____

_____

After Peter prayed, he turned to Dorcas' body and told her to get up. The Lord answered Peter's prayer and Dorcas opened her eyes and sat up. She was alive!

Imagine the thoughts running through the women's minds as they waited for Peter to reappear. What was he doing up there? How long would they have to wait?

Their waiting was well worth it. Rejoicing replaced the grief as Peter presented Dorcas to the widows and disciples - alive. Everyone in Joppa heard of the miracle.

What happened as a result of this news spreading throughout the town? (Acts 9:42)_____

_____

Lots of people in Joppa believed in the Lord. Following her salvation, Dorcas chose to make use of the talents and abilities she had been given to serve others and point them to Christ.

We have the same opportunity. The apostle Paul reminds us: "For we are his workmanship, created in Christ Jesus unto good works, which God hath before ordained that we should walk in them," (Ephesians 2:10).

Will you use the talents and abilities God has given you to serve others? Cultivate goodness in your life – it will point others to the Savior.

A Time to Reflect:

How does the Lord want you to respond?_____

_____

_____

_____

Prayer: *Heavenly Father, thank You for the selfless example of Dorcas and how she used her talents to serve others. Not only were her actions good, but they pointed to Your goodness. Help me be aware of the works that You've created me to do. Develop goodness in my life that will glorify You. In Jesus' name, Amen.*

Day 5

More than We Deserve

A Moment to Meditate & Memorize:

Finish memorizing this week's verse:

Psalm 107:8 Oh that men would praise the Lord for his goodness, and for his wonderful works to the children of men!

God's goodness can be seen in every area of our lives. He gives us life, is our constant companion, and loads us with blessings every day.

Today's lesson showcases His goodness in spite of our failures – big or small. Praise Him for this character quality.

A Life Lesson:

A bright flash of light followed by a deafening boom held me rooted to the spot. I could see a thick cloud of smoke pouring across the side yard; its acrid smell penetrating the house. Rain came down in sheets. Had lightning struck our home?

As I grabbed an umbrella and headed out into the storm, I expected to see flames shooting from the roof. My breathing slowed as I realized the house wasn't on fire. What a relief. But what had caused all that smoke earlier?

Back in the house, the smell of smoke was over-powering, and I noticed the power was out in a couple places. A quick trip downstairs to the breaker box remedied the power outage, but the smoke-smell remained a mystery. The odor seemed to be especially strong in the basement although I didn't see anything unusual.

Once my husband and I had a chance to check everything out, we calculated our losses. The invisible fence used to contain our dogs had been vaporized. Our cable, internet, and phone service had been knocked out. A power cord had been fried. And we finally figured out what had caused the smoke-smell.

When the lightning struck, electricity had traveled through the foundation of our house and exited through a couple metal pieces of exercise equipment we had in the basement. The force of the electrical current had literally torn and singed the rug underneath the equipment.

But instead of feeling grateful, I could only think of the cost of having to replace everything. I was tempted to complain. Why did the lightning have to strike so close to our house? This would be the second time we replaced the invisible fence this year. And what a headache to be without internet and cable service.

Over the next few days I heard stories about damage caused by lightning strikes – much more severe than what we had experienced. God was nudging me. He had protected us. I realized how fortunate we had been. No one had been hurt, our pets were safe, and there was no damage to the house.

Instead of choosing to complain, I should have chosen to praise Him for His protection. I didn't deserve God's goodness; but He extended it to me anyway and it had been evident all along.

What circumstances in your life have reminded you that God is good?_____

_____

_____

A Word from God's Word:

He was described as a man after God's own heart (Acts 13:22). With such an awe-inspiring testimony, it's hard to believe King David was capable of doing wrong. But strong temptation caused even this man to make a poor choice and fall into the grip of sin.

He should have been the one to lead his troops into battle. Instead, King David sent Joab to head up his army. Whatever his reason for staying behind, King David's decision opened the door to temptation that could have been avoided.

He found himself unable to sleep one evening and decided to take a stroll on the palace roof. While looking out over the city, something caught his attention.

What did King David see? (2 Samuel 11:2)_____

_____

Bathsheba was bathing on her rooftop – probably not the wisest decision. She was a beautiful woman and King David had definitely noticed.

Instead of averting his eyes and removing himself from temptation, King David allowed himself to enjoy the view and sent one of his servants to find out the identity of the lovely lady. He was the king after all. He had a right to know his subjects.

Temptation continued to hound King David even after he discovered that Bathsheba was married. He wasn't about to deny himself the pleasure of her company: "And David sent messengers, and took her; and she came in unto him, and he lay with her; for she was purified from her uncleanness: and she returned unto her house," (2 Samuel 11:4).

It wasn't long before word came that Bathsheba was pregnant. King David had Bathsheba's husband, Uriah, sent home in an attempt to cover his sin. He logically figured that Uriah would sleep with his wife and think the child was his. A perfect cover up.

But things didn't work out the way King David had planned. Uriah was a more loyal soldier than David had anticipated. He wouldn't think of going down to his house while his captain and fellow soldiers were sleeping in tents in the open fields.

What did King David decide to do? (2 Samuel 11:15)_____

_____

_____

He had Uriah positioned at the front of an extremely fierce battle, knowing he would be killed. Now King David was free to take Bathsheba as his wife. Everything would work out just fine. But David couldn't hide his sin from the Lord.

God sent Nathan the prophet to confront King David. He told a story about a rich man and a poor man. The poor man had nothing but one, highly-cherished lamb. When a visitor arrived at the rich man's house, instead of preparing a meal from one of the lambs in his flock, he sent and took the ewe lamb from the poor man.

King David's outrage was evident. How could the rich man be so heartless? David blurted out a harsh sentence. Nathan waited for a split second before leveling his accusation: "Thou art the man," (2 Samuel 12:7).

The Lord had blessed David with everything including the kingdom. David had given in to temptation and allowed wicked thoughts to lead to unthinkable actions.

How did King David respond? (2 Samuel 12:13)_____

_____

_____

He acknowledged his sin and asked for God's forgiveness. Being reminded of God's goodness led David to repentance.

God's goodness is evident in all of our lives. When we give in to temptation, let God's goodness lead you to ask forgiveness for your sin. He extends grace – which is way more than we deserve.

A Time to Reflect:

How does God want you to respond?_____

_____

_____

_____

Prayer: Heavenly Father, thank You for reminding me of the importance of resisting temptation. When I have wrong thoughts and I act on them, they will lead to sin. Thank You for Your goodness toward me even when I make poor choices. It's Your goodness that leads me to repent. In Jesus' name, Amen.

Questions for Group Discussion:

1. Life isn't easy. According to Psalm 107:8, where should our attention be centered when times get tough?

2. Where does material wealth come from? (Deuteronomy 8:18) Where should our focus be? (Matthew 6:19-20, 33)

3. We all face temptations. What does the Lord promise to do when we are tempted? (1 Corinthians 10:13) Share a victory you've experienced when faced with the opportunity to sin.

4. List the activities you're involved in. Evaluate them based on eternal significance. Does anything need to change?

5. It's hard to imagine a godly guy like King David committing sins like adultery and murder. Although there were consequences for David's sins, how did God demonstrate goodness to him? (2 Samuel 12:13)

Week 7

Faith: Striving to Hear "Well Done"

A faithful person is considered to be consistently loyal and conscientious, unwavering in his or her beliefs, and not adulterous. Do these words describe the average Christian? This week's lessons will take a look at demonstrating faithfulness in many areas of life. Get ready to be challenged!

This week at a glance:

Day 1 – *Kindred Spirits*

Day 2 – *Beyond the Vow*

Day 3 – *Using it All*

Day 4 – *Egypt & a Lion's Den*

Day 5 – *Forever Faithful*

Day 1

Kindred Spirits

A Moment to Meditate & Memorize:

We'll be studying faithfulness this week. Read through the verse several times and begin committing it to memory.

Matthew 25:21 His lord said unto him, Well done, thou good and faithful servant: thou hast been faithful over a few things, I will make thee ruler over many things: enter thou into the joy of thy lord.

In a day when living for self is the norm, faithfulness can be hard to come by. But this fruit of the Spirit has the power to leave a lasting impression. Read today's lesson and let the Spirit cultivate this characteristic in you.

A Life Lesson:

I remember meeting Darlene after a home school meeting. Our daughters were in the same group and we were pleasantly surprised to find out we lived in the same subdivision. A friendship was formed.

Our girls would get together to play and Darlene and I would go over the latest Beth Moore Bible study. Sharing prayer requests and praying for our families became a regular part of the week. I valued Darlene's friendship.

Our relationship was taken to a whole new level after I got in a car accident. When I began experiencing anxiety and started to withdraw from others, Darlene offered a listening ear. Because of her experience with others who had gone through anxiety, she continued to reach out to me.

My husband was traveling a lot at the time and irrational fears would plague me. Darlene made herself available even when it wasn't convenient for her. She would rearrange her schedule and come over to help me work through the concern I was grappling with. I began questioning God, and had a difficult time reading His Word.

With anxiety, I experienced sleepless nights and a lack of appetite. Darlene took me to lunch and encouraged me to continue pursuing my relationship with the Lord. When she began teaching a Bible study, she invited me to be a part of it. I didn't feel up to being in a group study.

Instead of dropping the issue, Darlene made time to meet privately and go over each lesson with me. Although I was too self-absorbed to see it at the time, her faithfulness helped me through a very dark valley in my life.

She was much more than a fair-weather friend. She chose to be there for me when life didn't make sense. Her actions were an accurate reflection of someone walking in the Spirit.

The Lord was able to use Darlene to play a significant role in my recovery because she was willing to be a faithful friend.

Write about a time God encouraged you through the faithfulness of a friend:

_____

_____

_____

A Word from God's Word:

Their relationship was special. We're given a few sobering facts before getting a closer look at the bond between Ruth and Naomi.

Naomi and her family had moved to Moab due to a famine in their homeland, Bethlehem-judah. But things didn't go as planned. Naomi's husband died. Her sons both married women from Moab, but after ten short years Naomi's sons died as well. The loss of her family was devastating.

When Naomi heard that the famine was over in Bethlehem-judah, she decided to return; there was no reason to stay in Moab. Her daughters-in-law, Orpah and Ruth, were intent on making the journey with her. Naomi must have been touched by their display of love, yet she wasn't convinced they should go with her.

What line of reasoning did she use to convince the women to stay in their homeland? (Ruth 1:11-13)_____

_____

_____

Naomi knew she was beyond child-bearing years. She wouldn't be able to provide other sons for Orpah and Ruth to marry. It made the most sense for the young ladies to return to their families' homes and marry men from Moab.

Although Orpah didn't want to leave Naomi, she saw the logic in the advice. With tears streaming down her face, Orpah kissed her mother-in-law and started for home. But Ruth wasn't so easily swayed.

How did Ruth respond? (Ruth 1:16-17)_____

_____

_____

Ruth was determined to go with Naomi, and she pledged her faithfulness to her. Nothing but death could separate them, and even then Ruth wanted to be buried in the same land as Naomi.

Ruth kept her word. When the two women arrived in Bethlehem-judah, Ruth took on the responsibility of taking care of her mother-in-law. She was determined to put food on the table and wasn't too proud to take advantage of the Jewish custom that allowed the poor to follow after those who worked in the fields and pick up the grain left behind. By evening she should have enough food for a meal.

When Naomi found out that Ruth had been gleaning in Boaz's fields, she praised the Lord. Only the hand of God could lead Ruth to the field of a man who was related to them.

Naomi was well-acquainted with Jewish law: when a woman's husband died, she could marry a brother of her dead husband. Since Naomi didn't have a son for Ruth to marry, the closest relative of the deceased husband could marry the widow. Boaz could play the part of the kinsman-redeemer. There was hope.

When Naomi and Ruth left Moab, life was full of uncertainties. Ruth chose to remain faithful to her mother-in-law, and God took care of the rest.

How did the Lord bless Ruth for her faithfulness? (Ruth 4:13)_____

_____

_____

Boaz married Ruth and the Lord gave them a son, Obed.

Yield to the will of the Holy Spirit and allow the fruit of faithfulness to be evident in your life.

A Time to Reflect:

Is it difficult for you to remain faithful to others? How does the Lord want you to respond to the lesson today?_____

_____

_____

_____

Prayer: Heavenly Father, Your Word is an amazing teacher. Thank You for the examples of ordinary people who chose to live for You. I can't be faithful in my own strength. Help me be sensitive to the needs of others and submit to Your Spirit that Your fruit will be seen and You will be glorified. In Jesus' name, Amen.

Day 2

Beyond the Vow

A Moment to Meditate & Memorize:

Review this week's verse and continue memorizing it.

Matthew 25:21 His lord said unto him, Well done, thou good and faithful servant: thou hast been faithful over a few things, I will make thee ruler over many things: enter thou into the joy of thy lord.

Faithfulness in marriage is commendable. As an extension of love, it stands the test of time regardless of the circumstances.

Choosing to do the right thing in spite of hardship can only be accomplished through the power of the Spirit. Allow Him to work in your life today.

A Life Lesson:

I watched his health decline. My dad had heart problems and underwent open-heart surgery when I was in fourth grade. Three years later he began experiencing extreme pain in his feet. What was initially considered gout was later diagnosed as rheumatoid arthritis: a difficult blow for my parents to handle.

It had to be hard for my mom to watch him suffer. My dad was a smart man; a research biologist for a large global chemical company. Now everything was put on hold. While he had made major contributions to his department at work and had provided a good living for us, a big question mark stood in the path of his future. My mom was there at his side. She chose to be faithful.

My brother and I were aware that my dad was sick, but we had no idea how it might affect us. I'm sure my parents spent many late nights talking about it. How would they make ends meet if my dad could no longer work? My mom had worked part-time for many years as a kindergarten teacher. She was willing to trim the budget and find additional work if it became necessary.

As my dad's disease progressed and he missed more and more work, medical disability became his only option. His weekly take-home pay was cut significantly, but because of my mom's financial savvy, my brother and I never noticed.

My mom was accustomed to hard work. She grew up on a farm with lots of responsibilities and was out on her own at the age of thirteen. It was no surprise that she took on a lot of the chores around the house when my dad was no longer able to do them.

My parents had set aside a college fund for my brother and I, and they expected us to make a contribution as well. But I remember my mom picking up a few cleaning jobs just to make sure we had enough money for our books. She was dedicated to our family.

When a situation is difficult, our human tendency is to scream for an escape. My dad suffered for many years with pain I can only imagine. Although my mom couldn't take away his pain, she didn't run away from the situation. Instead, she did what she could: chose to be faithful in practical ways that pointed to the Savior.

"Moreover it is required in stewards, that a man be found faithful," (1 Corinthians 4:2). My mom's devotion was a living example of faithfulness in action.

Write about someone who has been an example of faithfulness to you:_____

_____

_____

_____

A Word from God's Word:

She's thought of as the ideal woman. More than half a chapter in the Bible is devoted to this nameless female. She serves as an inspiration to each of us to be the woman God created us to be. I'm talking about the Proverbs 31 woman.

She's described as being virtuous; she has moral integrity. Her faithfulness in marriage is clearly seen.

How does she treat her husband? (Proverbs 31:11-12)_____

_____

She treats her husband so well that he trusts her completely. He has confidence that she will remain true to him.

She is known as a faithful worker. Her work ethic is admirable. She wants to be productive and isn't afraid of hard work: "She seeketh wool, and flax, and worketh willingly with her hands," (Proverbs 31:13).

Sometimes it's challenging to serve our families; especially when it requires getting up early. The woman found in Proverbs 31 gives us another glimpse of faithfulness in action; this time serving those in her household.

What does she do for her family members? (Proverbs 31:15, 27) _____

_____

_____

This lady is willing to get up early to prepare a meal for her family. And she does it without complaining. She makes sure everyone is taken care of and she avoids being lazy.

Generosity is also part of her nature. Notice her faithfulness to the poor.

Write out Proverbs 31:20_____

_____

_____

This verse confirms the Proverbs 31 woman's heart of compassion. She looks for ways she can supply the needs of the less-fortunate.

Her speech is something to be emulated. Because she is faithful to spend time with the Lord her words are filled with wisdom, and spoken with kindness.

Numerous examples of faithfulness are sprinkled throughout this passage of Scripture. By choosing to fear the Lord and submitting to His will, you can demonstrate the fruit of faithfulness just like the woman in Proverbs 31.

A Time to Reflect:

How does the Lord want you to respond today?_____

_____

_____

_____

Prayer: *Heavenly Father, thank You for showing me so many ways I can demonstrate faithfulness. Forgive me when I'm unfaithful. Help me yield to the power of Your Holy Spirit working in me. Continue to mold me into the faithful woman of God You want me to be. In Jesus' name, Amen.*

Day 3

Using It All

A Moment to Meditate & Memorize:

Continue memorizing this week's memory verse.

Matthew 25:21 His lord said unto him, Well done, thou good and faithful servant: thou hast been faithful over a few things, I will make thee ruler over many things: enter thou into the joy of thy lord.

How do you use the things you've been given? Whether it's time, talents, or finances, what you do with them speaks volumes. Let today's lesson spur you on to be a faithful steward – using everything to make much of your Heavenly King.

A Life Lesson:

They're not missionaries or in full-time ministry. In fact, they would have you believe they're just ordinary people. But it's easy to see there's something different. If you spend any time with them, it comes through loud and clear: they have made a conscious decision to use their resources and abilities for God and his work.

Teaching classes, organizing women's functions, visiting missionaries on the field, and discipling people; this husband and wife team is fully committed to doing whatever it takes to encourage others and help them grow in their walk with Christ.

With the means to live lavishly, they've purposely chosen to live in a modest manner. They support the church ministries financially and are quick to help a family in need. I'm challenged by their example.

All too often I realize the depth of my selfishness. It rears its ugly head when I plan my day – coaxing me to take it easy when I need to be working. I battle it when I go to the store and choose to buy something for myself instead of the gift I should pick up for a friend. I recognize it when I'm late to choir practice because I hit the snooze button. Faithfulness is a choice.

I need to see things from God's perspective. He has given me the talents and abilities I have. He has provided me with health and financial resources. Everything I have is on loan from Him. It's my responsibility to use it in a way that will please Him.

Faithfulness doesn't happen by accident. It requires a conscious decision, a lot of effort, and the power of the Holy Spirit. We're all stewards of what the Lord has given us. Let's choose to be faithful: "Moreover it is required in stewards, that a man be found faithful," 1 Corinthians 4:2.

Think about how God has gifted you. In what areas do you need to be more faithful?_____

_____

_____

_____

A Word from God's Word:

Faithfulness is a characteristic that touches every part of life. From being consistently trustworthy and loyal to family and friends, to being conscientious with our finances, time, and talents; faithfulness is a trait that pleases our Creator.

But being faithful is challenging. Jesus knew we would struggle, so He gave us several practical examples of this quality in action.

Jesus began one story with four main characters: the master, and his three servants. The master was taking a trip. He met with his servants to share his plans and entrust them with his things while he was away.

What did he give each servant? (Matthew 25:15)_____

_____

_____

He gave the first man five talents. He gave the second servant two talents. And the third man received one talent. Each servant got a portion he could handle.

Think about it. This was a big responsibility. The master was counting on these men to use what he had given them to the best of their ability until he returned. What happened?

Two of the servants did a good job investing their resources and doubled their money. The servant with one talent didn't do so well.

Instead of making use of what he had been given, what did this man do? (Matthew 25:18)_____

_____

For whatever reason, the third servant decided to hide the money he had been given. He wasn't thinking about the day when his master would return.

But the day came: the master came back. He was eager to see how his servants were doing. How had they handled his money? He was impressed with the first servant – he had made five talents in addition to the five he'd been given. The second servant had equally impressive results. He had doubled his money, and was able to give the master a total of four talents. The master was pleased.

What did he say to these two servants? (Matthew 25:21, 23)_____

_____

_____

His words must have warmed their hearts, "Well done, good and faithful servant…" They had been counted faithful with the treasure he had entrusted to them.

I can only imagine what the third servant was thinking as he clutched the one talent he had so carefully hidden in the dirt. His palms were probably sweating as he considered what he would say to the master.

He didn't have to wait long. It was his turn to approach the master. The excuse tumbled from his lips – he knew the master was a tough man with high expectations. He explained that because he was afraid he had hid what the master had given him. The servant extended his hand, the one talent visible in his open palm.

How did the master respond? (Matthew 25:26-30)_____

_____

_____

The master wasn't pleased. Instead of making use of what had been given to him, this servant had wasted the opportunity he had been given. The talent was taken from him and given to the servant who had ten. The unfaithful servant was cast out.

The illustration is clear. The Lord has given each of us time, talents, and finances. How are we using these gifts? No matter what we've been given, it's important for us to use each gift faithfully so we have something to present to our Master when He returns. Imagine the reward of hearing Him say, "Well done, good and faithful servant…"

A Time to Reflect:

How does the Lord want you to respond today?_____

_____

_____

_____

Prayer: *Heavenly Father, thank You for the example of faithful stewardship found in Your Word. It's so easy to forget that everything I have is from You. Help me to use the time, talents, and finances You've given me to bring You maximum glory. Continue to grow the fruit of faithfulness in my life. In Jesus' name, Amen.*

Day 4

Egypt & a Lion's Den

A Moment to Meditate & Memorize:

Continue memorizing this week's verse.

Matthew 25:21 His lord said unto him, Well done, thou good and faithful servant: thou hast been faithful over a few things, I will make thee ruler over many things: enter thou into the joy of thy lord.

The thought of persecution for the sake of the gospel can be frightening. It's a reality the apostle Paul reminds us to expect: "But thou hast fully known my doctrine, manner of life, purpose, faith, longsuffering, charity, patience...Yea, and all that will live godly in Christ Jesus shall suffer persecution," (2 Timothy 3:10, 12).

When persecution comes, cling to the Lord's faithfulness and let Him exhibit this fruit in your life to a watching world.

A Life Lesson:

To many, the lives of God's people don't make sense. They are smart people with lots of talent - in line to be the next company presidents or professional athletes.

But in spite of these options, they have chosen to pursue the vision God has given them: to share His gospel with people steeped in religion, often in hostile parts of the world. They are missionaries.

I can only imagine the challenges that surround these missionary families. From raising monthly support, to learning a foreign language and embracing a different culture; the inconveniences they face are daunting.

I'm reminded of the stories my husband and I have heard in recent months. Each real-life experience is a picture of faithfulness in action. Faithfulness to the Lord Jesus Christ.

Some friends of ours are serving in Egypt – where eighty to ninety percent of the people are Muslim. Conditions have been volatile, and it's all too common to see riot police on the streets of Cairo, the nation's capital.

In spite of the unrest, this family returned to Egypt after a short furlough to the states. Their time state-side had been anything but easy. The wife experienced a miscarriage, the husband had an epileptic seizure, and their son was diagnosed with a rare condition that has caused tumors to grow on his brain.

We would have understood if they cancelled their plans to return to Egypt. They could have stayed in the states with family where safety wasn't an issue. They could have found a specialist to deal with their son's health needs. Instead, they chose to return to the work God had called them to in Egypt.

Even as we questioned their decision, God was already at work. When they began holding Bible studies, one of the ladies in attendance received Christ as her Savior. And there have been others who have expressed an interest in hearing the gospel.

God has used their faithfulness to be an inspiration to many. And the Lord has blessed them with fruit that will remain for eternity.

How are you demonstrating your faithfulness to God?_____

_____

_____

A Word from God's Word:

He could have gotten bitter. He was taken from Jerusalem in the prime of his youth and made to serve in the courts of the Babylonians. But long before he was taken captive, Daniel had decided to be faithful to the Lord.

Instead of following the accepted customs of the land, Daniel continued to do what would please God. And God blessed him, giving him favor with the king.

When King Darius decided to set up princes over his kingdom, his top choice was Daniel.

Why did Daniel seem to be the logical choice? (Daniel 6:3)_____

_____

The king noticed something in Daniel that was lacking in the other princes: Daniel had an excellent spirit.

But when someone is promoted, jealousy often follows. The others who had been overlooked for the position weren't going to give in without a fight. What could be done? Surely they could find something in Daniel's past to disqualify him.

What did they find? (Daniel 6:4)_____

They found absolutely nothing! Daniel's record of service was squeaky clean. If they were going to accuse him of anything, they would have to attack his loyalty to God. They came up with a plan: one that included the king, prayer, and a lion's den. A fool-proof combination.

They wasted no time approaching King Darius and getting on his good side. Their argument sounded convincing: since Darius was the king, wouldn't it make sense for a royal decree to be put into place that made it mandatory for everyone to make their petitions only to him for the next 30 days? It seemed all the presidents, governors, and princes of his kingdom supported this idea. What an ego boost! Those who disobeyed would be put in the lion's den. King Darius put the proposed law into practice.

How did Daniel respond? (Daniel 6:10) _____

_____

_____

He continued to do what he had always done. He left his windows open, got down on his knees three times a day, and faithfully prayed and gave thanks to God just like he had done before the king's decree.

It didn't take long for the presidents, governors, and princes to approach the king with the scandalous news that Daniel had broken the law. Their plan had worked flawlessly. King Darius was beside himself. Of course these men had tricked him into signing the decree out of jealousy. How could he have missed it?

Nothing could be done. The law of the Medes and Persians could not be altered. Daniel would have to be cast into the den of lions.

The king spent a sleepless night. Early the next morning, he ran to the lions' den and called out to Daniel: "O Daniel, servant of the living God, is thy God, whom thou servest continually, able to deliver thee from the lions?" (Daniel 6:20)

What was Daniel's answer? (Daniel 6:22) _____

_____

_____

God had sent his angel and shut the lions' mouths, so they were unable to harm Daniel. The king was overwhelmed. Daniel had been spared.

The men who had brought accusations against Daniel weren't so fortunate. King Darius commanded that they be thrown into the lions' den along with their wives and children. They met the fate they intended for Daniel.

Daniel's faithfulness to God made King Darius take notice. He put another decree into place. This time, the king ordered everyone to reverence the God of Daniel; the God who reigns forever, and is able to deliver and rescue.

Instead of fearing for his life, Daniel put his life in the hands of God and demonstrated the fruit of faithfulness.

A Time to Reflect:

How does the Lord want you to respond today?_____

_____

_____

_____

Prayer: *Heavenly Father, forgive me for the many times I've chosen to live for self instead of choosing to be faithful to you. No matter what you've called me to do, help me submit to the Spirit's work so the fruit of faithfulness will be developed in my life. In Jesus' name, Amen.*

Day 5

Forever Faithful

A Moment to Meditate & Memorize:

Finish memorizing this week's verse.

Matthew 25:21 His lord said unto him, Well done, thou good and faithful servant: thou hast been faithful over a few things, I will make thee ruler over many things: enter thou into the joy of thy lord.

God knows what He is doing. He is able to meet our needs far better than we can imagine. So with a track record of such faithfulness, why do we find ourselves doubting Him? Pause and consider today's lesson when your faith is in need of a boost!

A Life Lesson:

When I was hired as Director of Development for a pregnancy care center, I knew the Lord was up to something. The job involved raising funds by hosting special events and developing donor relationships.

Fundraising was nowhere in my formal training. My game plan included raising money with a variety of events, from teaching aerobics classes to selling Christmas cards. There was just one problem. It was MY plan. Over the course of four years, I discovered the Lord would supply the finances the Center needed when I followed His plan.

When funding trickled in after each fundraiser, I realized my strategy wasn't working. As the Executive Director of the Center and I prayed about the situation, we eliminated the unprofitable fundraising events, and decided to concentrate on one main activity: our annual Walk for Life. We then shifted our focus to cultivating relationships with our existing donors and with those who were potential donors.

The number of clients we saw and the programs we offered continued to grow; so in addition to money for the general budget, there was a special project we were also trying to fund – a new facility. We wanted to remain debt-free, so the plan was to pay cash for the new Center.

I have to admit I was skeptical. But God knew what He was doing. Every year we set aside a large percentage of the money we raised from the Walk for Life, and designated it to our special project.

Meanwhile, things were getting interesting in my personal life. I remember when the phone call came. A company in Georgia offered to buy my husband's business. We made the decision to accept their offer.

With my time coming to a close at the Center, it was difficult to step away from my job. I had hoped to complete the fundraising for the new facility.

I heard the news just a few days before we moved. One of our donors gave a sizeable gift toward the purchase of the facility we were considering. The building project we had been working on for four years would become a reality. God's timing left me speechless. I now felt comfortable leaving – the task was finished.

The doors of the new Center opened just four months after we moved. What a memorable display of God's faithfulness. "Now unto him that is able to do exceeding abundantly above all that we ask or think, according to the power that worketh in us, unto him be glory…" (Ephesians 3:20-21a).

How has God demonstrated His faithfulness to you?_____

_____

_____

_____

A Word from God's Word:

We can always rely on God. He is faithful – and He never changes. He keeps his promises.

Think about the children of Israel. They had been in bondage to the Egyptians for several hundred years. God had made a covenant with Abraham, Isaac, and Jacob years earlier. They would have many descendants and would possess the land of Canaan as an inheritance.

I imagine the Israelites had given up all hope of escaping the sting of the leather whips carried by their cruel Egyptian taskmasters. But God had not forgotten His people. He had heard their cries and sent a deliverer: Moses.

The promise of God to multiply the Israelites was already a reality, and now His promise to give them the land of Canaan was set in motion. With Moses leading the people, they faced their first challenge at the Red Sea.

How did God prove He was faithful? (Exodus 14:21-22)_____

_____

_____

The Lord told Moses to stretch out his rod over the Red Sea and it would be divided so the people could cross over on dry land. And just as God had said,

163

Pharaoh and his army would attempt to follow them and be swallowed up in the sea - never to be seen again.

Over and over the Lord provided for the people in the wilderness: He gave them water from a rock, He supplied them with food in the form of manna, He led them with a pillar of cloud during the daytime and a pillar of fire at night. Talk about miraculous provision.

He brought them to the very brink of the land He had promised them. But they refused to go in.

Why didn't they trust God? (Numbers 13:31-33)_____

_____

_____

 They were afraid of the people that inhabited the land. The children of Israel shrank back in fear and forgot about God's past faithfulness.

Before we judge them too harshly, don't we tend to be like those forgetful Israelites? We know God is with us, and we're grateful for the things He provides, yet we just don't know if we can trust Him when our backs are up against the wall.

Take a look at the 23rd Psalm.

Where does the Lord make us lie down, and where does He lead us? (v. 2)___

_____

_____

He makes us lie down in green pastures, and leads us beside still waters. When we face the difficult trials of life, He is right beside us. He can be trusted; we don't need to be afraid. There will be times when our enemies surround us, but the Lord offers His protection. And our final home will be with Him in heaven for eternity.

What a beautiful picture of the faithfulness of our God!

A Time to Reflect:

How does the Lord want you to respond today?_____

_____

_____

_____

Prayer: *Heavenly Father, thank You that Your mercies are new every morning, great is Your faithfulness (Lamentations 3:23). Help me be careful to recognize Your presence and provision in my life, and to remember them when I face hard times. Develop faithfulness in my life. In Jesus' name, Amen.*

Questions for Group Discussion:

1. How did God demonstrate His faithfulness to both Ruth and Naomi?

2. Which example of faithfulness from the woman in Proverbs 31 was most challenging for you? Why?

3. Is there an area where you could be a better steward of what God has given you? Commit the area to prayer and if you feel comfortable, share it with your group.

4. Daniel was faithful to God even when persecution came. Years before, he had purposed in his heart to remain true to God. How was his faithfulness rewarded?

5. How has God been faithful to you? Share specific examples with your group and conclude with a prayer of praise.

Week 8

Meekness: When Yielding is a Good Thing

Moses and the Lord Jesus Christ were both described as meek. Neither was weak. Each was willing to yield his will to the will of God the Father. The dictionary defines the term meek as gentle, tender; free from pride. The five lessons in this weeks' chapter will offer concrete examples of this character trait. Yielding to the will of God will allow the fruit of meekness to flourish in your life.

This week at a glance:

Day 1 – *No Need to Retaliate*

Day 2 – *A "Yes, Lord" Attitude*

Day 3 – *Being a Voice*

Day 4 – *Pouring it Out*

Day 5 – *Priceless*

Day 1

No Need to Retaliate

A Moment to Meditate & Memorize:

This week our topic is meekness. Read through the verse several times and meditate on it today.

Matthew 11:29 Take my yoke upon you, and learn of me; for I am meek and lowly in heart: and ye shall find rest unto your souls.

Have you ever gotten defensive when your reputation was at stake? Fortunately we don't have to go into defense mode if the Lord is our Savior. He stands for us. And a meek response gives glory to our great God.

A Life Lesson:

The opposite of being meek, is being prideful. Unfortunately, I'm no stranger to pride. When criticism comes my way, I feel the walls go up around my heart – forming an impenetrable barrier. Hurtful words bring pain and cause me to become defensive. I feel as if I've been attacked. Pride takes over.

I remember the brief article I wrote for a local website. My first eBook, God Speaking, had just been released and I was interested in publicizing it. The editor of the website approved my article and it was visible a few days later.

Not everyone was as excited about my eBook as I was. Someone left a comment accusing me of proselytizing, and felt the article had no place in the community news. My heart rate increased and pride pushed its way to the surface. What happened to freedom of speech? My article had been approved by the editor, hadn't it?

I decided to give myself a day or two before responding to the unkind comment. Reacting in anger wouldn't be the wisest thing to do. When I revisited the site a few days later, I was surprised to find the editor had posted a comment in my defense.

She addressed the person with respect, and explained that my article was listed under the "Local Voices" column, "Religion" category. She went on to say that bloggers who wrote for her had permission to publicize their books on the website. Her comment concluded by thanking the person for leaving a comment.

Wow. The editor had responded beautifully. She had defended me in a way that defused the whole situation. In short, she took responsibility for allowing the article to appear on-line, yet did it in a way that was professional and gentle.

I was reminded of the miracle of meekness. The meek person sets aside personal feelings, values the other person in spite of the situation, and allows the Lord to be magnified.

What did you learn about meekness today?_____

_____

_____

A Word from God's Word:

Moses didn't volunteer for the job. In fact, he made every excuse he could think of to get out of it. But the Lord had chosen him to approach Pharaoh and ask for the release of the children of Israel. They had suffered at the hands of the Egyptians for hundreds of years, and the Lord was ready to deliver them using Moses.

Moses witnessed the mighty hand of God in each of the plagues that rocked the land of Egypt – from lakes and rivers turning into blood, to the death of the firstborn of every Egyptian. I can only imagine the elation he and the Israelites felt as their captors begged them to leave Egypt. The God of the Israelites had proven He was more powerful than any of their gods.

Leading over a million people in the wilderness was no easy task. Moses constantly turned to God for answers. The people had a bad habit: they were complainers. They grumbled about the lack of water. They griped about the food. They even found fault with their leader, Moses.

Aaron and Miriam were Moses' brother and sister. Aaron was privileged to be Moses' spokesperson, and Miriam ministered to the women. But at some point, jealousy crept in and these two began criticizing Moses.

How does the Bible describe Moses? (Numbers 12:3)_____

_____

He was very meek – more so than any other man on the earth. That's pretty meek! So when Aaron and Miriam's complaints about Moses' leadership began, Moses didn't even have to defend himself. God stepped in and took up for him, questioning their boldness to speak against His faithful servant.

Siblings weren't the only ones to challenge Moses' leadership. Some of the men, who were given positions as workers in the tabernacle, began grumbling against his authority too. Korah, Dathan, and Abiram headed up a group of 250 men intent on proving their superiority to Moses.

How did Moses respond when they became jealous of his position? (Numbers 16:4-5)_____

_____

Instead of arguing, Moses fell on his face and sought God's counsel. It would have been easy for Moses to demand their allegiance. After all, God had put him in this position. But over and over again, Moses went to bat for the children of Israel who continued to whine and complain about his leadership.

Moses didn't let his position go to his head. Because he was intimately acquainted with the God who had entrusted him to be a leader, he was able to remain humble, and demonstrate a meek spirit.

Allow the Lord to defend your reputation and develop the fruit of meekness in your life.

A Time to Reflect:

Have you confused meekness with weakness? How does the Lord want you to respond to the lesson today?_____

_____

_____

_____

Prayer: *Heavenly Father, thank You for the life of Moses and how he demonstrated meekness. Teach me to rely on You to defend my reputation when I'm tempted to retaliate. Help me grow in grace and in the knowledge of You so I can live a life filled with meekness. In Jesus' name, Amen.*

Day 2

A "Yes, Lord" Attitude

A Moment to Meditate & Memorize:

Begin memorizing the verse for this week.

Matthew 11:29 Take my yoke upon you, and learn of me; for I am meek and lowly in heart: and ye shall find rest unto your souls.

How do you respond when the Lord directs you to do something difficult? Moving forward in obedience isn't always easy. A meek spirit will help you develop the right attitude – one that answers, "Yes, Lord."

A Life Lesson:

Her sweet spirit was the first thing I noticed. Corli and her husband, Kevin greeted our group at the airport in Port Elizabeth, South Africa. They had been missionaries to the Xhosa people for eight years. They knew we would be exhausted and had arranged for my husband, Steve and me to stay at a local bed and breakfast while on our first mission trip.

Although we had never met, Corli's kindness and hospitality made us feel right at home. She filled us in on some of the cultural differences we could expect; her soft-spoken words causing us to lean forward in our seats. A large gift basket was waiting for us when we got to the bed and breakfast – every snack imaginable carefully placed inside.

In addition to teaching at several church services in the townships, our group also had the opportunity to see some of the amazing sights of South Africa. Whether we were interacting with the Xhosa people, or traveling from one place to another, I was struck by Corli's servant heart.

With two small children in tow, she still managed to interact on a meaningful level with the ladies in her women's group, and be a gracious hostess. We were shocked to hear of the large number of stateside church groups who visited every year.

Kevin and Corli were used to opening their home to host these groups; offering them a place to stay and serving up delicious home cooked meals. I wasn't sure I'd be able to handle running a mini-hotel, but Corli knew this was part of their ministry and seemed to thoroughly enjoy it.

Toward the end of our trip, as we discussed their ministry, I asked Corli how I could pray for her. After spending a week with her, it came as no surprise when she requested prayer for her and her husband to be humble servants. It was clear to me this was one request she prayed about often. And the Lord was answering.

I came away having learned a lot in our brief time in South Africa. One of the beautiful things that challenged me was the meekness evident in the life of a missionary-wife named Corli. She was a living example of gentleness, tenderness, and an absence of pride. She had yielded her will to the Lord and He was able to use her in a mighty way.

How have you seen meekness displayed in the life of someone you know?____

_____

_____

A Word from God's Word:

She was betrothed to Joseph. Like every bride-to-be, I'm sure Mary was counting down the days until the wedding celebration. There were preparations to be made, and an entire lifetime with her husband to look forward to.

It was probably a routine day in the city of Nazareth. Mary may have been absorbed in her morning chores, when suddenly she was no longer alone in the room. She heard a voice and tried to make sense of what was being said.

The angel spoke to her: "Hail, thou that art highly favoured, the Lord is with thee: blessed art thou among women," (Luke 1:28). What kind of greeting was this? What did he mean? Mary was troubled. But he was speaking again.

What news did the angel share with Mary? (Luke 1:30-31)_____

_____

_____

She had found favor with God; she had been chosen to be the mother of the promised Messiah, Jesus! He would be great and would reign over the house of Jacob – His kingdom would never end.

Unbelievable. To be chosen to bear the very Son of God! The information must have sent Mary's head spinning. But she was having a hard time connecting the pieces. How could she have a child when she was a virgin? It didn't make sense.

How did the angel answer Mary's question? (Luke 1:35)_____

_____

She would become pregnant by the power of the Holy Ghost. Incredible.

A young unmarried girl who became pregnant faced harsh consequences. It was possible that Mary's father would disown her. Since the child wasn't Joseph's, Mary risked losing him as well. There was no doubt she would be excluded from society.

Mary didn't stop to consider what might happen. Her response was swift and wholehearted.

What did Mary say to the angel? (Luke 1:38)_____

_____

_____

"Behold the handmaid of the Lord; be it unto me according to thy word," (Luke 1:38). What beautiful words of submission. Instead of focusing on the risks she faced, Mary set her gaze on doing the Lord's will. He had asked her to serve Him in this unusual way, and she was willing to lay aside the plans she had for her life in order to be an obedient servant.

By choosing God's will above her own, Mary displayed great meekness. Choose God's will today and cultivate this valuable fruit of the Spirit.

A Time to Reflect:

How does the Lord want you to respond to the lesson today?_____

_____

_____

_____

Prayer: *Heavenly Father, thank You for showing me Mary's meekness. Instead of pausing to think about what might happen to her, she traded her will for Yours. Teach me to be that kind of servant. Grow the fruit of meekness in my life. In Jesus' name, Amen.*

Day 3

Being a Voice

A Moment to Meditate & Memorize:

Continue memorizing the verse for this week.

Matthew 11:29 Take my yoke upon you, and learn of me; for I am meek and lowly in heart: and ye shall find rest unto your souls.

Pride is not a characteristic linked with meekness. Self takes a backseat while priority is given to others. The Lord is magnified when we step out of the way and point people to Him. Be encouraged by the lesson today.

A Life Lesson:

He loves his job. The Associate Pastor at our church has an enthusiasm that's contagious. Steve and I have been privileged to serve at the same church with him, his wife and kids for the past few years.

I remember feeling slightly awkward as we walked into the church as visitors for the first time. Pastor Trent was there to greet us. He showed a genuine desire to get to know us and quickly put us at ease. His passion for the Lord couldn't be missed, and it was clear he wanted to make a difference in the community.

As we continued visiting the church, Pastor Trent made a point to get to know Steve and me. He would ask Steve how business was going, and he showed an interest in my writing.

Recently, we were able to attend a blessing service to honor Pastor Trent and his family for their years of service at the church. One character trait was mentioned repeatedly: humility. His main objective is to magnify King Jesus. And he lives his life displaying the servant-attitude of Christ.

Person after person shared how Pastor Trent had been there for them. He had no selfish motives, just a desire to help each person succeed. A true spirit of meekness. From giving others the opportunity to teach a Sunday school class, to attending a teenager's special event, his life has clearly made a lasting impression.

Pastor Trent is passionate about getting the gospel to those who don't know Christ as their personal Savior. He has a special burden for the country of India – a country steeped in false religion.

He and his wife had the opportunity to go to India, not for a vacation, but for the sole purpose of creating a documentary to raise awareness of the great need for the gospel in that place. Pastor Trent worked with some men from another organization, Brandon and Eric, to capture footage that would accurately show the need of the people.

Long hours spent in the heat in less than ideal conditions greeted them, but Pastor Trent wasn't thinking of himself. His thoughts were far different: "I was moved greatly. I had much more liberty to sit, talk, and contemplate but Brandon and Eric were always working on something to make sure that what our hearts were capturing was also going to be captured on film. They worked very hard for God's glory and for the good of this project. Their soft hearts but diligent focus is going to be used by God on this project and I am certain on many more to come."

Pastor Trent's example challenges me to love the Lord with all my heart and to put others' needs before my own. That's what meekness looks like in action.

What step will you take today to demonstrate meekness?_____

_____

_____

A Word from God's Word:

His purpose was determined by God before he was born. John the Baptist would prepare the people for the coming of Christ. He was different than the rabbis of the day. He wore clothing made of camel's hair and his diet consisted of locusts and wild honey. Not your typical teacher.

Even as John began his ministry, many of the Jews had questions. They sent priests and Levites to find out who this unusual preacher claimed to be. Was he the promised Messiah?

How did John answer? (John 1:20)_____

_____

He said he was not the Christ. His answer baffled them. If not the Christ, then who was this man? Maybe Elijah, or one of the prophets? But he denied it. Who then? John's answer was plain: "I am the voice of one crying in the wilderness, Make straight the way of the Lord, as said the prophet Esaias," (John 1:23).

Although he was only one man, John was using all he had been given to point others to Christ. His focus was not on himself, but on the One who would come after him. His job was to prepare the people to follow the Messiah.

There was no doubt in John's mind that Jesus was the Son of God. As he baptized many in Bethany, John testified to the holiness of the One who would come.

What did John say about Jesus? (John 1:27)_____

_____

_____

Jesus was the preferred One. The One they had been waiting for. John said he was unworthy to be Christ's servant – he wasn't even fit to untie the Lord's shoelaces. John knew his place. John demonstrated meekness.

The very next day John witnessed Jesus coming toward him. Instead of drawing attention to himself, John invited everyone to look to Jesus: "Behold the Lamb of God, which taketh away the sin of the world. This is he of whom I said, After me cometh a man which is preferred before me: for he was before me," (John 1:29-30).

In a time when his ministry was thriving, John encouraged his disciples to leave and follow Jesus instead. John understood his mission and was satisfied to be the voice who prepared the way for Christ's ministry.

Sum up how John lived his life using the words from John 3:30: _____

_____

He must increase, but I must decrease (John 3:30). Words that describe the life of someone submitted to the will of the Lord Jesus Christ. Embrace a life filled with this characteristic – the quality of meekness.

A Time to Reflect:

How does the Lord want you to respond to the lesson today? _____

_____

_____

_____

Prayer: Heavenly Father, thank You for showing me what meekness looks like in action. Forgive me for the many times I've been more concerned about building a name for myself than pointing others to You. Help me submit as You develop the fruit of meekness in me today. In Jesus' name, Amen.

Day 4

Pouring it Out

A Moment to Meditate & Memorize:

Continue memorizing the verse for this week.

Matthew 11:29 Take my yoke upon you, and learn of me; for I am meek and lowly in heart: and ye shall find rest unto your souls.

Although the term "servant-leadership" is well-known, successfully putting it into practice can be another story. Serving others first with a gentle, tender mindset is God-inspired. After reading today's lesson, think about who you can serve.

A Life Lesson:

She's one of those people you can depend on. My sister-in-law, Stephanie, is a talented author with a big heart for the Lord and for others. She doesn't miss an opportunity to share a word of encouragement, or to offer help when it's needed.

I remember when our daughter, Riley, was a baby. She had a severe case of stranger anxiety. Steve and I hesitated to leave her, knowing she would cry and get all worked up in the short amount of time we would be gone.

Family functions gave Riley the opportunity to get used to relatives while we were in close proximity. Stephanie would offer to entertain Riley while Steve and I grabbed a quick bite to eat. It wasn't long before Stephanie had formed a bond with our girl.

Stephanie volunteered to watch Riley on several occasions when I worked outside the home. Her gentle spirit and tender heart won Riley over completely. A couple years later, when I enrolled Riley in a Bible study where Stephanie was a teacher, Stephanie did some juggling behind-the-scenes to ensure our girl would be in her group. It made all the difference for Riley and gave me peace of mind every time I dropped her off for her class.

Years later, it was Stephanie's encouragement that prompted me to begin writing. She was busy writing a book, but was willing to step away from her agenda to read and critique my work – offering valuable insight that led to my first published article. Her humble attitude made me aware of the quality of meekness in her life.

I'm not the only one who has been on the receiving end of Stephanie's generosity. I've noticed she's quick to pour herself into the lives of others. Spending time with nieces and nephews, encouraging friends with a quick text or message, and putting feet to the practical things that help others are just a handful of the way she ministers.

The way Stephanie has chosen to live her life doesn't come naturally. It's an inner working of the Holy Spirit that shows up as precious fruit – the fruit of meekness. You'll experience a harvest of this fruit in your life as you pursue God's will for your life instead of your own.

Write about an example of meekness from your own life: _____

_____

_____

A Word from God's Word:

What comes to mind when you think of a king? Maybe you picture a highly visible head of state with a specific agenda, or someone who lives in a castle or palace. Whatever your mental image, it probably doesn't include someone who is willing to submit to the will of another. Kings make the rules, they don't bow to others.

There was one King who was different. His birth was announced by angels. Jesus could have been born in a palace; instead He chose a crude stable. From the beginning He knew His kingdom was not physical but spiritual. He was well aware of His purpose.

Why did Jesus come to earth? (Luke 19:10)_____

_____

He came to seek and to save the lost. Although He was God, Jesus set aside His divine rights and privileges, and became a man. He humbled himself out of obedience to the Father and served others. He embodied meekness.

As a 12-year old boy, Jesus was already focused on His mission. He had traveled to Jerusalem with His parents, relatives, and friends for the feast of the Passover. When the celebration ended, everyone headed home – everyone except Jesus. He stayed behind at the temple; listening to the teachers and asking them questions.

When Mary and Joseph realized Jesus was missing from their group, they began a frantic search. Where could He be? They found Him sitting with the teachers in the temple. Mary scolded Him for staying behind.

How did Jesus respond? (Luke 2:49)_____

_____

He told them He had to be about His Father's business. Jesus understood He was the Son of God. But He willingly returned to Nazareth with Mary and Joseph and was obedient to them.

Years later, when Jesus began His public ministry, He traveled from city to city preaching and healing the sick. Not everyone embraced His message. Many refused to repent of their sins and believe in Him as their Messiah. While Jesus renounced those cities, He prayed for people in other cities who were searching for relief from their heavy burden of sin. If they would come to Him, He promised to give them rest.

Jesus used the illustration of a yoke to help people understand His desire to help them. Just like a yoke keeps oxen close together and divides the workload, Jesus wanted them to get into the yoke He provided, so they would stay close to Him and allow Him to assist them. Jesus' described His yoke as easy and said His burden was light.

If someone got in the yoke with Jesus, what would he/she learn about Him? (Matt. 11:29)_____

_____

_____

Jesus was gentle and humble – a Savior characterized by meekness. At the final Passover He shared with His disciples, Jesus continued to serve. The custom was for a servant to wash the feet of the guests assembled for the feast.

What did Jesus do? (John 13:5)_____

_____

He poured water in a basin and washed the disciples' feet. He set the example for His disciples to serve others. Jesus continued to display meekness even when the time came for Him to be crucified. In the garden of Gethsemane, knowing what was before Him, Jesus agonized in prayer to His Heavenly Father.

What did He say? (Luke 22:42)_____

_____

_____

Jesus asked for the cup of suffering to be removed from Him, but wanted the Father's will above His own. He was willing to submit to the Father's will in order to redeem mankind – an unmistakable example of meekness.

As you stay in the yoke with Christ, the Holy Spirit will develop this fruit in your life.

A Time to Reflect:

How does the Lord want you to respond to the lesson today?_____

_____

_____

_____

Prayer: Heavenly Father, Your Word is life and light. Thank You for the beautiful examples of meekness that characterized Your Son, Jesus. Help me remember Your kingdom principles are different than those of the world. In Your economy, serving others is important. Letting go of my will and embracing Yours will help me develop the fruit of meekness in my life. In Jesus' name, Amen.

Day 5

Priceless

A Moment to Meditate & Memorize:

Finish memorizing the verse for this week.

Matthew 11:29 Take my yoke upon you, and learn of me; for I am meek and lowly in heart: and ye shall find rest unto your souls.

We may not talk about meekness as much as love, joy, and peace – but this fruit of the Spirit is just as important. Let the Lord put His finger on wrong attitudes and actions in your life. Follow His will and not your own, and meekness will prevail.

A Life Lesson:

Parenting is not for the faint of heart. Our precious babies don't come home from the hospital with a manual addressing every situation we'll experience over the next 21 years. But the Bible gives us instructions for training our children and cautions us not to discourage our kids by provoking them.

I've made my fair share of mistakes as a parent. My quick temper and harsh words have made a mess of several teachable moments. Even when I've blown it as a mom, the Lord has been faithful to remind me that all is not lost. Although I may not have handled the situation correctly, I have the opportunity to say two far-reaching words, "I'm sorry."

Apologizing goes against my nature. I don't like to admit I'm wrong. But the Holy Spirit's nudge reminds me that righteousness trumps right every time. When I agree with Him, and humble myself, He's able to develop the fruit of meekness in my life.

I remember a time when I needed to apologize to my daughter Riley. She had asked me if I was mad at her. In reality, I was angry – I just wasn't aware that I was letting it show. Her question caught me off guard and I did what I shouldn't have done: unloaded every reason why I was perturbed with her behavior. I'm sure I included some things that weren't even relevant.

Although there were some issues I needed to address, I didn't do it in the right spirit. I did so in anger without the intention of restoring her. It was time for me to get alone with the Lord.

The Lord put His finger on the pride in my heart and I knew I had to make things right. I apologized for my outburst and re-visited the matters that had irritated me in the first place.

Riley accepted my apology and we were able to pray about the issues together. The beautiful thing about asking forgiveness is the restoration and peace that follows. Living in the power of the Holy Spirit makes it possible to grow in meekness.

How is the Holy Spirit developing the fruit of meekness in your life?_____

_____

_____

_____

A Word from God's Word:

Meekness is valued by God. Jesus showed us what this character trait looked like when He walked on earth. From the moment He laid his power and glory aside and took on flesh, an unmistakable humility was obvious in this One who was both God and man.

Never has gentleness, tenderness, and an absence of pride been more evident than in the life of our Savior. Although He was the King of kings, He chose to do things far differently than the kings of his day.

How did Jesus enter Jerusalem? (Zechariah 9:9; Matthew 21:5)_____

_____

_____

Jesus entered the city exactly as it had been foretold by the prophet Zechariah over 500 years earlier: on a donkey's colt, meek and lowly.

Fast forward to the crucifixion. Instead of spewing out words of hatred at those who mocked Him, Jesus prayed for His Father to forgive them. He endured the excruciating pain and humility of the cross because He chose to submit to the Father's will. Meekness characterized both His life and death.

Jesus wants us to live our lives following His example. Several promises are linked to living a life of meekness.

What does Psalm 25:9 say?_____

_____

Because of their humble attitude, the meek are teachable and the Lord can guide them in justice. These people aren't know-it-alls. They realize their need for God and His direction in their lives.

The Lord supplies the needs of the meek. The Psalmist David noted the everyday provisions as well as those to follow in eternity: "The meek shall eat and be satisfied: they shall praise the Lord that seek him: your heart shall live for ever," (Psalm 22:26).

When we allow the Holy Spirit to perfect this fruit in our lives, what does the Lord say He will do? (Psalm 147:6)_____

_____

He will lift us up and cast the wicked down. Jesus emphasized this concept in one of many discussions with the Pharisees of His day: "For whosoever exalteth himself shall be abased; and he that humbleth himself shall be exalted," (Luke 14:11).

The promises of God are not limited to this lifetime. Some of the rewards of meekness are still to come. God's Word speaks of the meek inheriting the earth (Matthew 5:5, Psalm 37:11). When Christ is reigning in the future, this promise will be fulfilled.

What is priceless in the sight of God? (1 Peter 3:3-4)_____

_____

_____

Someone who has a meek and quiet spirit. Someone who is in tune with Him. It's important to place the right emphasis on the fruit of the Spirit the Lord values.

A Time to Reflect:

How has your view of meekness changed as a result of this week's lessons? How does the Lord want you to respond to the lesson today?_____

_____

_____

_____

Prayer: Heavenly Father, thank You for the perfect example of meekness in the Lord Jesus Christ. I can't produce meekness in my own strength. Help me rely on the Spirit to grow this fruit in my life. Thank You for the wonderful promises related to meekness. Help me live for You today. In Jesus' name, Amen.

Questions for Group Discussion:

1. Define meekness. How did your thoughts about this fruit of the Spirit change after reading this week's lessons?

2. What did Mary risk by having a "Yes, Lord" attitude? How did the Lord bless her obedience?

3. What verse accurately sums up how John the Baptist lived his life? Commit this verse to memory.

4. Have you found Christ's yoke to be easy and light? Why or why not?

5. Give examples of meekness from Jesus' life. What promises are given to the meek?

Week 9

Toughing it out with Temperance

Self-control is desperately needed today. In a society that applauds an 'if it feels good, do it' mentality, temperance seems to be extreme. This chapter will highlight the benefits of a self-controlled lifestyle, and challenge the reader to walk in the Spirit to avoid the temptations of an undisciplined way of life.

This week at a glance:

Day 1 – *Sexual Intimacy: Worth Waiting For*

Day 2 – *Time Well-Spent*

Day 3 – *Sleep & an Army of Ants*

Day 4 – *Selfless Service*

Day 5 – *Give the Spirit Control*

Day 1

Sexual Intimacy: Worth Waiting For

A Moment to Meditate & Memorize:

Temperance is better known as self-control or restraint. Read through this week's verse and meditate on it today.

Galatians 5:16 This I say then, Walk in the Spirit, and ye shall not fulfil the lust of the flesh.

Promiscuity is nothing new. Since the beginning of time, the devil has worked to make the sacred things of God commonplace. The physical intimacy God intended to be shared between husband and wife has been exploited by the deceiver as something to be enjoyed by any two consenting people.

Let today's lesson reassure you that temperance in this area is not old-fashioned – it's God-honoring.

A Life Lesson:

I met her when she was in junior high. She came from a difficult background. Her father had been killed in a motorcycle accident, leaving her mother to provide for her and her brother.

Because of her mom's work schedule, she was often at home alone – a situation that led to problems as she got older. I was caught off guard when she voiced her concern. She couldn't have been more than fourteen years old. She was worried that she might be pregnant.

Having worked as a hotline volunteer at a pregnancy care center, I shouldn't have been shocked. I had answered calls from females of all ages with similar concerns. Society's lies and human nature had tempted these girls to give in to premarital sex. They had decided that self-control was out-dated.

Instead of drawing the relationship closer together as it does in marriage, sex often drove these couples apart: leaving shattered lives, and often an innocent baby to further complicate things.

Fortunately, the pregnancy care center offered programs that pointed back to the Author of Life and His plan and timing for intimacy. The Father's love was shared with each girl. Support groups and material resources were available to the girls who were pregnant. Abstinence programs were discussed with those who were single and had a negative pregnancy test.

The abstinence education program was a vital part of the ministry. It consisted of a series of skits put together by co-directors who then recruited Christian students to perform them in local schools. The truth about God's plan for sex was clearly presented. A single question was raised by attendees over and over: "How is it possible to remain abstinent?"

The Christian students were able to share their relationship with Jesus Christ, and how the power of the Holy Spirit made it possible for them to say no to sex outside of marriage. Temperance wasn't so old-fashioned. When a young person was committed to being self-controlled, it opened the door for a wonderful marriage relationship in the future.

How have you seen self-control displayed in the life of someone you know?__

_____

_____

_____

A Word from God's Word:

They were struggling. The believers in Corinth were tempted on every side by the immorality in their culture. Sex and prostitution were a normal part of the false religions in their city. It wasn't long before decadent behavior crept into their church.

The apostle Paul confronted their sin in a lengthy letter. Just because the people could ask forgiveness for their sins, it didn't give them license to do whatever they pleased. There was a deeper problem here.

Paul reminded the Corinthian believers that they were new creatures in Christ. They shouldn't be taking their cues from society. Salvation had set them free. They were set free **from** sin, not set free **to** sin. Paul was very blunt.

What did he tell the Corinthians? (1 Corinthians 6:13b)_____

_____

_____

The Lord hadn't given them their bodies for the purpose of fornication. They were to use their bodies to serve the Lord.

God created every human being with a body, soul, and spirit. What was done with the body would affect the soul and spirit. They couldn't commit sexual sin and still maintain a close relationship with the Lord.

God wasn't against physical intimacy; in fact He had given sex as a special gift to mankind. But it was to be enjoyed by a husband and wife **only** within the confines of marriage. The unmarried Corinthian believers were to exercise self-control. Submitting to the power of the Holy Spirit would make it possible.

Surrounded by a promiscuous society, the church members in Corinth were challenged by the words of Paul. He told them the truth.

What did he say to the believers? (1 Corinthians 6:19)_____

_____

_____

Paul reminded them that their bodies were the temple of the Holy Ghost. They weren't to live as if they were unaccountable for their behavior. What they did mattered. Temperance was important.

Each of the believers had been bought with a price. It wasn't an inexpensive transaction. The very Son of God had given His life as a ransom to pay their sin debt. He had endured agony. His body had been beaten unmercifully. He suffered the humility of the cross. The precious blood of Jesus Christ had been shed to pay their sin debt and give them eternal life.

Those who had accepted Christ as Savior were mocking the sacrifice that had cost the Redeemer His life.

What did Paul tell them to do? (1 Corinthians 6:20)_____

_____

_____

Glorify God in their body and spirit because they belonged to Him.

Temperance was an issue in Paul's day just like it is in our own. It **is** possible to overcome sexual temptation. Remember who you belong to, and say yes to the Holy Spirit as He develops the fruit of self-control in your life.

A Time to Reflect:

How does the Lord want you to respond to the lesson today?_____

_____

_____

_____

Prayer: Heavenly Father, I'm constantly amazed at the relevance of Your Word for my life. People in Paul's day struggled with sexual temptation just like people do today. Thank You for showing me how to exercise self-control. Help me remember I belong to You. In Jesus' name, Amen.

Day 2

Time Well-Spent

A Moment to Meditate & Memorize:

Begin memorizing this week's verse.

Galatians 5:16 *This I say then, Walk in the Spirit, and ye shall not fulfil the lust of the flesh.*

Time is a precious commodity. Once it's spent it is impossible to reclaim. Do you spend your time wisely? Prioritize time with the Savior – it will be time well-spent.

A Life Lesson:

My morning routine is pretty straight-forward: feed the pets, exercise, eat breakfast, and do my Bible study. I leave plenty of time for writing, and household chores. There are two things that can sabotage my day – not scheduling my time, and failing to account for interruptions.

Believe it or not, sometimes it's more challenging to get things done when I have fewer things scheduled. Temperance is not at the forefront of my mind. With no appointments to keep and just a couple articles to write for the day, it's easy to squander time. Social media, email, and current events vie for my attention. Sometimes I give in. What about you?

When I take the time to schedule things on my calendar, I'm much less likely to give in to the time-wasters. I remember the importance of being a good steward of the time I've been given and tend to accomplish so much more. It's easier to live with the mindset of Moses who authored the 90th Psalm: "So teach us to number our days, that we may apply our hearts unto wisdom," (Psalm 90:12).

There isn't a day that goes by without an interruption of some sort. Whether it's a phone call or an unanticipated visitor, I've come to realize it's wise to plan a little extra time for these unexpected breaks. Many times I've found them to be divine interruptions orchestrated by God to keep me mindful of His ultimate control of my schedule.

I remember the trip to the grocery store I'd carefully worked in between my final writing assignment and heading off to church. There weren't many items on my list, so I knew I'd be in and out of the store quickly. God's plan was a little different.

As I unloaded my groceries at the cash register, the clerk struck up a conversation with me about one of my purchases. I mentioned that I was taking some food to our mission conference. She began telling me the story of her husband who had recently accepted Christ as His Savior.

Her situation had been difficult for a number of years. Her face lit up when I offered to pray for her and her husband. Encouraging someone in the Lord was far more important than accomplishing everything on my to-do list that day.

Write about a time when you chose to honor God with your schedule:_____

_____

_____

_____

A Word from God's Word:

Without phones or email, they probably weren't anticipating His visit. But when Jesus arrived in Bethany, the two sisters, Mary and Martha, were more than happy to welcome Him into the home they shared with their brother Lazarus.

Jesus' public ministry kept Him very busy, and He was often thronged by followers. It must have been quite an honor to have Jesus stop by for a visit. After the customary greeting, the two sisters headed in different directions.

What did Mary do? (Luke 10:39)_____

_____

Mary found a place at Jesus' feet – eager to hear what He had to say.

I can imagine what Martha must have been thinking. Her mind was focused on serving their guest. What refreshments were on hand to offer Jesus? Without refrigeration or fast food restaurants, anything she came up with would have to be prepared by hand – a time consuming process.

I'm sure Martha came up with a plan and was already putting it into motion when she realized Mary was still sitting at the feet of Jesus. Why wasn't Mary helping her? Martha felt as if the burden of serving had fallen entirely on her shoulders. Something had to be done. Martha's irritation must have been evident as she approached Jesus.

What did Martha say to Jesus? (Luke 10:40)_____

_____

_____

She blamed Jesus for not caring that she was serving alone, and asked Him to tell Mary to help her! While Jesus didn't scold Martha for desiring to serve Him, He used the opportunity to teach an important lesson.

How did Jesus respond to Martha? (Luke 10:41-42)_____

_____

_____

While Martha was distracted with all the details that went into serving Jesus, Mary had chosen to use her time in a more profitable way: listening to the Lord.

It's easy to get focused on serving the Savior when the most important thing is spending time in His presence. Allow the Holy Spirit to develop temperance in your life so you'll be a good steward of the time you're given.

A Time to Reflect:

Do you use your time wisely? How does the Lord want you to respond to the lesson today?_____

_____

_____

_____

Prayer: *Gracious Heavenly Father, thank You for the gift of time. Forgive me when I waste the time You've given me. Help me grow in self-control, and help me choose to spend time with You every day. In Jesus' name, Amen.*

Day 3

Sleep & an Army of Ants

A Moment to Meditate & Memorize:

Continue memorizing this week's verse.

Galatians 5:16 *This I say then, Walk in the Spirit, and ye shall not fulfil the lust of the flesh.*

No matter what form our daily responsibilities take, the Lord has given each one of us 24 hours to accomplish them. Aside from the necessities like eating and sleeping, how do you spend your time? Let today's lesson from the ant teach you an important truth about temperance.

A Life Lesson:

I'm not the earliest riser. Because I don't work a job outside the home, it's easy to get tripped up by the temptation to be lazy. When the alarm goes off, I've got a decision to make: stay under the warmth of the covers, or make good use of the new day God has given me.

The Lord continues to use my journey as a writer to help develop the fruit of temperance in my life. I remember discussing this very Bible study with my husband a few years ago over dinner at Golden Corral. At the time, I imagined it as a nine book study: one book devoted to each characteristic of the fruit of the Spirit.

As I began doing a bit of research and finally started writing the study, it seemed like a formidable task. After much counsel and a few writing classes, my plan shifted significantly from what I had originally envisioned.

Instead of attempting to write a series of studies, I'd focus on writing a single study with one chapter devoted to each character quality associated with the fruit of the Spirit. Even with the project trimmed down significantly, I lacked motivation. Shorter writing assignments offered me convenient reasons to postpone this particular project. I got lazy.

I'm the type of person who enjoys an assignment with a complete list of instructions, rather than a blank canvas without rules. Writing a Bible study seemed like a daunting challenge. Several weeks and months passed before I realized nothing would get accomplished on my project if I didn't begin writing.

Accountability in the form of a critique group started the ball rolling. I committed to finishing a lesson each month to share at the writers' group. At that rate, it would take me 50 months to finish my study. The Lord made me aware of chunks of time throughout the day that I could be putting to better use. I began writing a lesson every week.

When I finally established a completion date and made it public, I realized the Holy Spirit was helping me become more self-controlled. It was possible for me to get up earlier, finish the articles I was responsible for, and still have time to write an additional lesson for my Bible study.

Admitting that I had been lazy was the first thing I needed to do before I could see how the Lord wanted me to move forward. Self-control didn't come naturally. I was able to grow in temperance as I yielded to the will of the Father.

How has the Lord developed temperance in your life?_____

_____

_____

A Word from God's Word:

We can learn a tremendous amount from God's creation. Even the tiniest creatures can teach us big lessons – the ant is no exception.

Although this insect is often thought of as a nuisance, God designed ants with some characteristics that should cause us to sit up and take notice. The Master Creator invites us to take a close look at the ant's behavior.

What do we stand to gain when we observe the ant? (Proverbs 6:6)_____

_____

We can gain wisdom. Wikipedia's description of the ant opens our eyes to some valuable traits: "Ant societies have division of labour, communication between individuals, and an ability to solve complex problems," (http://en.wikipedia.org/wiki/Ant).

Did you notice the ant is a hard worker? Every insect in the colony has a job to do. They know what they are to do and they do it. Laziness is a non-issue. They provide us with an excellent example of temperance.

Describe the ant's work ethic: (Proverbs 6:7-8)_____

_____

_____

These bugs are amazing. They don't have a boss, or anyone giving them directions, yet they work as a team to gather and store up food for their colony. When it comes to humans, this type of work ethic would make a pretty big impression on those around us.

But let's face it; it's tempting to be lazy. It's easy to hit the snooze button on the alarm instead of embracing the day and all it has to offer. Those few extra moments of sleep are delicious when compared to another workday.

What does the Lord warn us about? (Proverbs 6:9-10)_____

_____

_____

It isn't wise to sleep instead of working. We need to exercise self-control, understanding that God has provided us with a job to do so we can take care of ourselves and our families.

What happens to those who give in to laziness? (Proverbs 6:11)_____

_____

These people will become poor. They don't give any thought to providing for the needs of today or those they will have in the future. All this can be avoided by practicing temperance.

Is the Lord suggesting that we never sleep? Of course not. He knows rest is important. For the Jews in the Old Testament, God instituted the Sabbath which was a weekly day of rest. Our bodies were designed to be refreshed by sleep.

What does God say about sleep in Psalm 127:2?_____

_____

_____

It's useless for us to stay up and work all the time. It's important to find the balance between working hard and trusting God to provide for our needs.

Allow the Lord to develop the fruit of temperance in your life so you can apply yourself to the work He has for you instead of giving in to laziness.

A Time to Reflect:

How does the Lord want you to respond to the lesson today?_____

_____

_____

_____

Prayer: *Heavenly Father, I admit that I sometimes give in to laziness. Forgive me. Thank You for the example of the ants and how they work diligently without oversight from a boss. Help me choose to do the work You've given me to do instead of choosing to be lazy. Grow the fruit of temperance in my life today. In Jesus' name, Amen.*

Day 4

Selfless Service

A Moment to Meditate & Memorize:

Continue memorizing the verse for this week.

Galatians 5:16 *This I say then, Walk in the Spirit, and ye shall not fulfil the lust of the flesh.*

It's easy to get stingy with time. We view it as something we can control. But do we consider how God wants us to use the time he's given us? Whether it's time, abilities, or resources – we're wise to exercise temperance.

A Life Lesson:

Steve and I have enjoyed getting to know a sweet family at our church. They love the Lord, and are involved in many ministry opportunities.

I think back on the transition periods my husband and I have gone through every time we've relocated and joined a new church. Change is never easy and it can provide just the right excuse to stay on the sidelines. It's tempting to sit back and observe rather than jumping in to help.

That's not the case with this family. Their example has provided me with a lesson in temperance. They've made the conscious decision to use the abilities God has given them and spend time serving – even when it means working behind the scenes.

Cleaning the church facility isn't a very glamorous job. Yet, soon after becoming members, our friends volunteered to be added to the monthly cleaning schedule. The dad, mom and two girls viewed it as an opportunity to do something for the Lord together.

I still remember seeing them come into the building early on a Saturday morning to clean. I knew what it was like to give up the only opportunity to sleep in on a weekend. To my shame, it had taken me over a year to commit to attending music practice on Saturday mornings. That was my time to get a little extra rest and do some things around the house. I knew I should be using the musical ability God had given me, but for a long time I justified my decision to stay home.

A desire to be selfish with my time was tough to resist. This family's example caused me to reconsider. The truth? Time and talent weren't mine to begin with – they were gifts from the Lord. I should be talking to Him about how He wanted me to use them.

Our friends also embraced opportunities to lead prayer time, greet visitors, work in the nursery, and teach the Bible. Their involvement at church challenged me, but I knew their dedication to Christ reached far beyond the walls of the church building.

Although they're not in full-time ministry, they were willing to use their abilities and extra time to make a difference in the local church. What a beautiful demonstration of self-control.

How have you exercised temperance with the talents and abilities God has given you?_____

_____

_____

A Word from God's Word:

We don't know a lot about them. Aquila and Priscilla were a husband and wife team mentioned only five times in the Bible. Although we're not given many details about this couple, the information that's shared leaves little doubt that this man and woman practiced temperance in their daily lives.

When the ruler of Rome commanded the Jews to leave his city, Aquila and Priscilla moved from Italy to Corinth.

What was this couple's occupation? (Acts 18:3)_____

_____

Because they were tentmakers, Aquila and Priscilla were able to take their business with them when they moved. Young Jews were taught a trade that would allow them to earn a living. The apostle Paul was also a tentmaker.

On one of his journeys to Corinth, Paul stayed with Aquila and Priscilla. We're not told much about the time they spent together, but clearly Paul had quite an influence on them. While they continued to make tents to pay for the essentials, they made a decision to do something that may have been considered radical.

What did Aquila and Priscilla choose to do? (Acts 18:18)_____

_____

They joined Paul on a missionary journey to Syria! This wasn't like a mission trip today. There were no airplanes to catch, or daily itineraries to follow. Aquila and Priscilla left the comfort and safety of home to sail with Paul to a foreign country and share the gospel.

I can only imagine what must have been going through Priscilla and Aquila's minds. How long will we be gone? Will it be a dangerous journey? We'll really miss our friends and church family.

Although they may have had similar questions and concerns, this couple chose to accompany Paul and resisted the temptation to stay behind where things were comfortable. They exercised temperance.

As they travelled with Paul, Aquila and Priscilla couldn't miss his passion to strengthen the believers no matter where he went. Having such an enthusiastic example left its mark on this husband and wife team.

What did they do when they heard Apollos preaching in the synagogue? (Acts 18:24-26)_____

_____

_____

They realized that although Apollos was a fervent believer, he was only familiar with the teachings of John the Baptist. They willingly invited him to spend time with them so they could teach him more about Jesus Christ. Aquila and Priscilla were committed to investing in the lives of others and not using their time selfishly.

I'm not sure where they ended up settling after their travels with Paul. One thing is certain; they continued to serve the Lord.

What did Aquila and Priscilla begin in their home? (1 Chorinthians 16:19)__

_____

They started a church – no easy task. This ordinary couple was willing to use their time and talents in a way that would make an eternal difference. What an encouraging example of self-control in action.

How could you exercise better self-control with your time and talents?_____

_____

_____

A Time to Reflect:

How does the Lord want you to respond to the lesson today?_____

_____

_____

_____

Prayer: Heavenly Father, thank You for these examples of temperance. I admit that sometimes I'm selfish with the resources You've given me. Please forgive me. Help me be self-controlled in my use of the time and talents I've been given. In Jesus' name, Amen.

Day 5

Give the Spirit Control

A Moment to Meditate & Memorize:

Finish memorizing the verse for this week.

Galatians 5:16 *This I say then, Walk in the Spirit, and ye shall not fulfil the lust of the flesh.*

When we're treated poorly, it's tough not to retaliate. With Christ as our Savior, it's His example we follow: "Who, when he was reviled, reviled not again; when he suffered, he threatened not, but committed himself to him that judgeth righteously," (1 Peter 2:23).

Let today's lesson encourage you to give the Spirit control in life's most challenging situations.

A Life Lesson:

No one is perfect. But my friend's example spoke volumes. Her self-control in a difficult relationship made an impact on my life.

They were the type of couple who seemed to have everything going for them. In my mind, promising careers, a nice house, close-knit family and friends, and the fact that they were believers should have added up to 'happily ever after.' Unfortunately, real life got in the way.

I remember getting the phone call. The news was devastating. My friend and her husband were having problems; there was another woman in the picture. I could only imagine the humiliation and defeat my friend must have been feeling.

Instead of lashing out in anger at the man who had betrayed her, she stuck with the facts and chose her words carefully. Her self-control was evident. She was willing to fight for their marriage. She chose to practice tough love, asking him to move out of their house and get counseling.

Throughout their separation she was willing to work on their marriage. It paid off. After several months, my friend told me she and her husband were reunited. They were slowly working through trust issues, but were back on the right track.

Unfortunately, not all separations end so well. Another friend in different circumstances ended up going through a painful divorce. It wasn't her choice to end the marriage, but instead of trying to retaliate and punish her former husband, my friend chose to pray for him. I knew the Holy Spirit was at work in her life – the fruit of temperance was easy to see.

Difficult relationships aren't uncommon; but responding to them in a God-honoring way can pose a challenge. Allow the Holy Spirit to guide your words and actions. The result will be a life filled with temperance.

How do you respond when someone hurts or offends you?_____

_____

_____

A Word from God's Word:

He was being hunted like an animal. David had been wary of King Saul for months. Ever since the people had made a big deal about David's victory in battle, he noticed a difference in Saul's behavior.

What had originally seemed like jealousy had become much more intense. Was it possible that he was in danger? After dodging the king's javelin on more than one occasion, David knew the answer.

What did David do? (1 Samuel 21:10)_____

_____

He found himself running for his life. But when David reached Adullam he was no longer alone. A large group of men willingly placed themselves under David's leadership and became his faithful army. Ever mindful to stay one step ahead of King Saul, David and his men moved from place to place.

In between battles, Saul was constantly searching for David. His men kept him informed of David's whereabouts. Following a skirmish with the Philistines, Saul found out that David was in the wilderness of En-gedi. Saul wasted no time paying him a visit.

But the visit didn't go exactly as Saul had planned. David and his men just happened to be in the cave Saul chose to enter. With his men encouraging him to kill the king, David's actions may have shocked them. He didn't even try to hurt Saul, but simply cut off the edge of his robe.

What was the reason David spared King Saul? (1 Samuel 24:6)_____

_____

_____

He refused to kill Saul because the Lord had anointed him king over Israel. David showed great respect for Saul's position, and even referred to him as "my master." Instead of exacting revenge for Saul's mistreatment of him, David exercised great self-control.

David was willing to reason with Saul. He told the king it was pointless to pursue him because he posed no threat. For a time Saul stopped following David.

The reprieve didn't last long. Saul and three thousand of his best soldiers once again began searching for David. When word got back to David that Saul was in the area, he and one of his men, Abishai went to investigate. Sure enough, Saul's army was pitched nearby.

Under the cover of darkness the two crept into Saul's camp. Abishai's advice sounded familiar, "God hath delivered thine enemy into thine hand this day: now therefore let me smite him, I pray thee, with the spear even to the earth at once, and I will not smite him the second time." His men continued to think that killing the king was the answer.

How did David respond? (1 Samuel 26:9-11)_____

_____

_____

He told Abishai not to kill him. The Lord had anointed Saul as king and would not hold the man guiltless who took his life. David was confident that the Lord would remove Saul from the throne in His timing. Wow – David once again chose to react with self-control.

In situations where it seemed like David had a right to take the life of the king, he chose not to. It would have been easy to justify his behavior, but instead he demonstrated temperance in extremely difficult circumstances.

How will you exercise self-control in a challenging relationship?_____

_____

_____

_____

A Time to Reflect:

How does the Lord want you to respond to the lesson today?_____

_____

_____

_____

Prayer: *Heavenly Father, thank You for reminding me that self-control is possible even in situations with difficult people. I'm grateful for the examples from the life of David. Help me choose temperance even when people around me justify the decision to take revenge. Help this fruit of the Spirit grow in my life. In Jesus' name, Amen.*

Questions for Group Discussion:

1. As a believer, our body is not our own. Who does our body belong to, and how should we use it? (1 Corinthians 6:19-20)

2. Do you schedule quiet time with the Lord as part of your daily routine? Choose someone from your discussion group as an accountability partner to keep you on track in this area.

3. Define lazy. What can you learn from observing the ant? (Proverbs 6:6-11)

4. What did you learn from reading about the lives of Aquila and Priscilla? What changes do you need to make in your life concerning your time and talents?

5. Exercising self-control in a difficult relationship is proof of the Spirit at work in your life. Spend some time in prayer for those who have wronged you.

Week 10

Knowing It + Putting It into Practice

=

An Abundance of Fruit

The Lord wants us to produce fruit: love, joy, peace, longsuffering, gentleness, goodness, faith, meekness. The good news is that He doesn't expect us to do it on our own. When we allow Christ to live through us, the Holy Spirit does the work.

This chapter will review each characteristic of the fruit of the Spirit and challenge you to live a life submitted to the Lord. The result will be spiritual growth and an abundance of fruit.

"Ye have not chosen me, but I have chosen you, and ordained you, that ye should go and bring forth fruit, and that your fruit should remain…" (John 15:16a).

This week at a glance:

Day 1 – *You Can't Do It Alone*

Day 2 – *Love & Joy: An Overview*

Day 3 – *Peace & Longsuffering: A Final Review*

Day 4 – *Looking Back: Gentleness, Goodness & Faith*

Day 5 – *A Final Look at Meekness & Temperanc*

Day 1

You Can't Do It Alone

A Moment to Meditate & Memorize:

Read through this week's verse several times and meditate on it today.

Galatians 5:22-23 But the fruit of the Spirit is love, joy, peace, longsuffering, gentleness, goodness, faith, meekness, temperance: against such there is no law.

I'm so thankful the Lord didn't expect me to produce these nine characteristics on my own. How freeing to realize it's not the fruit of Maria, but rather the fruit of the Spirit – His power working through my yielded life – that puts these traits on display to showcase the Father.

So what do you say? Let's submit to Him this week and take a final look at the fruit He will cultivate in our lives.

From My Heart to Yours:

Congratulations! Can you believe we've made it to Week 10? We've considered all nine characteristics of the fruit of the Spirit. By now, you can probably name each one of them: love, joy, peace, longsuffering, gentleness, goodness, faith, meekness, temperance.

A life that produces lots of fruit doesn't happen by accident. Every day I have a choice: to attempt to accomplish things in my own strength, or to realize my inadequacy and lean on the strength of the Lord.

Writing this study has helped me come to face to face with this very weakness: trying to produce something spiritual on my own. The truth is I can't. My Heavenly Father graciously waits for me to acknowledge Him and let the Holy Spirit do the work – He alone can produce a harvest of fruit that will remain.

The fruit of the Spirit is always in style. But there's no getting around it, this type of fruit is noticed the most when circumstances are out of control and the pressure is on.

Let's be honest, it's not particularly difficult to demonstrate love when you and your spouse are on the same page and the kids are behaving. It's when your husband offends you, and the kids won't listen to your advice that the test begins. Will you try to handle these situations on your own? Or will you call on the power of the Holy Spirit?

I know from experience, if I don't rely on the Holy Spirit, my tongue will get me into all kinds of trouble. I'll say things I'll later regret, and my anger will get the best of me. You too?

Don't get discouraged. The Lord is well acquainted with our weaknesses, and His Holy Spirit can help us grow an abundance of spiritual fruit.

"Ye have not chosen me, but I have chosen you, and ordained you, that ye should go and bring forth fruit, and that your fruit should remain:" (John 15:16a).

That's His prayer for you. And it's mine too. Prepare for a fruitful life!

A Word from God's Word:

Salvation frees us from the grip of sin and clothes us in the righteousness of Christ. Relying on the power of the Holy Spirit makes it possible for us to live a life that is pleasing to the Lord. We are able to produce fruit that points others to the Savior.

When teaching his followers, Jesus often used stories and parables to illustrate spiritual truths. Sometimes His words were hard to comprehend. But the disciples had no problem understanding the story of the husbandman in his vineyard.

God the Father was the husbandman and Jesus was the vine. And there were several branches attached to the vine.

What happened to the branches? (John 15:2)_____

_____

The branches that didn't bear fruit were taken away and those that produced fruit were pruned. Although cutting the branches away from the plant seemed counterproductive at first, the action encouraged fuller growth and caused the branches to bear more fruit.

The disciples could see the application. As He preached and taught, Jesus often pointed out the things that were hindrances in the lives of the believers. If they allowed Him to prune these things – although painful at first – they would be able to produce something of eternal value: a harvest of good fruit.

It was clear that the Lord wanted to use them to draw others to Him. But self-effort couldn't get the job done.

How was it possible to produce the fruit Jesus was talking about? (John 15:4)

_____

_____

Just like a branch could only produce fruit when it was connected to the vine, they could only produce fruit by abiding in Christ. The illustration made perfect sense.

Pruning caused something pleasing to replace a negative characteristic. When trials came, the right action and attitude would be on display. Love would be visible instead of hatred. Patience would be practiced instead of intolerance. Kindness would reign in the place of rudeness.

Good fruit produced in the midst of difficulties would be impossible to miss. To forgive the person who had slandered them would cause others to stop and take notice. To pray for those who beat them would certainly get people's attention. These things would be possible by staying connected to the source of power: Jesus Christ.

When Jesus ascended to heaven, whom did He promise to send to all believers? (John 16:7)_____

_____

He would send the Comforter – the Holy Spirit. The Holy Spirit would give the believers understanding of the things that Christ had taught: He would glorify the Father.

After Jesus' ascension, the early believers lived fruitful lives. This harvest brought glory to the Father. It's no different today. The Lord intends for us to bear fruit. Stay close to Him and let the Holy Spirit produce a bountiful harvest in your life.

A Time to Reflect:

How does the Lord want you to respond to the lesson today?_____

_____

_____

_____

Prayer: Heavenly Father, thank You for setting me free from the grip of sin and filling me with the power of the Holy Spirit. I want to abide in You so I can produce a harvest of fruit that will bring glory to You. In Jesus' name, Amen.

Day 2

Love & Joy: An Overview

A Moment to Meditate & Memorize:

Begin memorizing this week's verse.

Galatians 5:22-23 *But the fruit of the Spirit is love, joy, peace, longsuffering, gentleness, goodness, faith, meekness, temperance: against such there is no law.*

Love and joy are probably the most familiar characteristics of the fruit of the Spirit. As you consider these traits today, allow the Lord to speak to you and be obedient to His leading.

A Time to Review:

Take a few minutes to review Week 1, *Is It Love?*

Summary: Love goes far beyond the dictionary definition – to feel tender affection or desire for somebody (Encarta Dictionary). Love gives without expecting anything in return. The Bible describes the traits that characterize love: kindness, a longsuffering nature, humility, not envious, not boastful, not easily angered, rejoices in the truth, bears all things, believes all things, hopes all things, and endures all things. Love never fails.

Spend some time in prayer. Ask the Lord if you demonstrate biblical love. Ask Him to bring these characteristics of love to mind as you interact with people today.

What one statement or verse in these lessons on love was most meaningful to you?_____

_____

_____

What specific step does the Lord want you to take to develop the fruit of love in your life today?_____

_____

_____

_____

Look over Week 2, Jesus, Others, You: The Right Way to Spell Joy.

Summary: Joy is an attitude of the heart that is not dependent on circumstances. It flourishes when we put Christ first in our lives and leads to rejoicing.

Spend some time in prayer. Ask the Lord to show you the difference between happiness and joy. Ask Him to fill you with His joy.

What one statement or verse in the lessons on joy was most meaningful to you?_____

_____

_____

What specific step does the Lord want you to take to develop the fruit of joy in your life today?_____

_____

_____

_____

Prayer: *Heavenly Father, thank You for speaking to me through Your Word. I want my life to be characterized by love and joy. Help me rely on Your Holy Spirit for the right responses when life gets messy. Let others see You. In Jesus' name, Amen.*

Day 3

Peace & Longsuffering: A Final Review

A Moment to Meditate & Memorize:

Continue memorizing this week's verse.

Galatians 5:22-23 But the fruit of the Spirit is love, joy, peace, longsuffering, gentleness, goodness, faith, meekness, temperance: against such there is no law.

Peace and longsuffering don't come about by chance. Today's lesson will encourage you to review these traits and continue abiding in Christ so they will be evident in your day to day life.

A Time to Review:

Review Week 3, *A Different Kind of Peace.*

Summary: Peace goes far beyond an absence of conflict. We will experience trials and struggles in this life, but peace can reign in our hearts when we realize Christ has overcome the world. The Lord is our source of peace.

Pray about this topic. Ask the Lord to help you identify worry in your life. Ask Him to calm your heart today and be your Prince of Peace.

What one statement or verse in the lessons on peace was most meaningful to you?_____

_____

_____

What specific step does the Lord want you to take to develop the fruit of peace in your life today?_____

_____

_____

_____

Look over Week 4, *Hang in There: The Art of Suffering Long.*

Summary: Longsuffering can be defined as patient endurance in the face of suffering. We're not eager to sign up for hardship, but when others see this fruit of the Spirit in action, they can't miss the Savior.

Spend some time in prayer. Ask your Heavenly Father to give you patience when you experience trials. Realize others are observing your life; ask the Lord to give you strength for the things you'll encounter today.

What one statement or verse in the lessons on longsuffering was most meaningful to you?_____

_____

_____

What specific step does the Lord want you to take to develop the fruit of longsuffering in your life today?_____

_____

_____

Prayer: *Heavenly Father I know You're at work. It's only through Your power that I can have peace in a sinful world, and patiently endure things I would never have chosen for myself. Thank You for continuing to produce the fruit of the Spirit in my life. In Jesus' name, Amen.*

Day 4

Looking Back: Gentleness, Goodness, & Faith

A Moment to Meditate & Memorize:

There's still time to memorize this week's verse.

Galatians 5:22-23 But the fruit of the Spirit is love, joy, peace, longsuffering, gentleness, goodness, faith, meekness, temperance: against such there is no law.

Jesus Christ is the supreme example of gentleness, goodness, and faithfulness. As believers, we're clothed in His righteousness – able to respond in a way that pleases Him when faced with temptation. Praise Him today.

A Time to Review:

Review Week 5, *Journey to Gentleness.*

Summary: Gentleness is responding to others with kind and mild treatment. The power of the Holy Spirit makes this possible even in the most difficult situations.

Pray about this topic. Ask the Lord to help you identify times when you've been harsh or rude. Seek His wisdom and direction before you respond to others today.

What one statement or verse in the lessons on gentleness was most meaningful to you?_____

_____

_____

What specific step does the Lord want you to take to develop the fruit of gentleness in your life today?_____

_____

_____

_____

Review Week 6, *The Battle Between Good & Evil.*

Summary: God is 100% good. When we submit to the Holy Spirit, we are able to have the mind of Christ: replacing evil thoughts with good thinking.

Pray about this topic. Ask the Lord to give you discernment where your thoughts are concerned. Ask Him to help you take every thought captive so you can obey Him and think right thoughts.

What one statement or verse in the lessons on goodness was most meaningful to you?_____

_____

_____

What specific step does the Lord want you to take to develop the fruit of goodness in your life today?_____

_____

_____

_____

Take a look at Week 7, *Faith: Striving to Hear, "Well Done"*

Summary: The Bible defines faith in Hebrews 11:1: "Now faith is the substance of things hoped for, the evidence of things not seen." We can be unwavering in our beliefs and consistently loyal through the help of the Holy Spirit.

What one statement or verse in the lessons on faith was most meaningful to you?_____

_____

_____

What specific step does the Lord want you to take to develop the fruit of faith in your life today?_____

_____

_____

_____

Prayer: *Heavenly Father, it's impossible for me to grow any spiritual fruit on my own. Thank You for the gift of the Holy Spirit who is able to help me choose to be gentle, good, and full of faith. Help me submit to His power as I go through life today. In Jesus' name, Amen.*

Day 5

A Final Look at Meekness & Temperance

A Moment to Meditate & Memorize:

Finish memorizing this week's verse.

Galatians 5:22-23 But the fruit of the Spirit is love, joy, peace, longsuffering, gentleness, goodness, faith, meekness, temperance: against such there is no law.

We've come to the end of the study. Today we'll review the final two traits of the fruit of the Spirit mentioned in Galatians 5:23 – meekness and temperance. As you yield more and more of your life to the Holy Spirit, you'll experience a fruitful harvest that will bring joy to the Savior. God bless.

A Time to Review:

Review Week 8, *Meekness: When Yielding is a Good Thing.*

Summary: Meekness is not weakness. In fact, it's characterized by a humble, gentle and submissive spirit. The term meek denotes an attitude free from pride.

Spend some time in prayer. Ask the Lord to point out times when you've been anything but meek. Ask your Heavenly Father to give you a meek spirit when you're tempted to respond with pride today.

What one statement or verse in the lessons on meekness was most meaningful to you?_____

_____

_____

223

What specific step does the Lord want you to take to develop the fruit of meekness in your life today?_____

_____

_____

_____

Take a look at Week 9, *Toughing it out with Temperance.*

Summary: Temperance is defined as self-restraint in the face of temptation or desire (Encarta Dictionary). Simply put, temperance is self-control.

Spend some time in prayer. Ask the Lord to show you the areas where you struggle with self-control. Ask the Lord to help you stand firm when you're tempted today, and to practice this fruit of the Spirit.

What one statement or verse in the lessons on temperance was most meaningful to you?_____

_____

_____

What specific step does the Lord want you to take to develop the fruit of temperance in your life today?_____

_____

_____

_____

Prayer: *Heavenly Father, thank You for reminding me that through Your power I have the ability to demonstrate meekness and temperance. As I come to the end of this study, I know the key to producing spiritual fruit is by staying connected to You – like a branch to the vine. Help me choose to submit to You one day at a time. Use my life to grow spiritual fruit that will last and make an eternal difference. In Jesus' name, Amen.*

Questions for Group Discussion:

1. When we try to produce the fruit of the Spirit in our own strength, what happens? How is the fruit of the Spirit produced? (John 15:5)

2. What area do you need to yield more fully to produce an abundance of love and joy? Write out a verse that will help you and refer to it often (i.e. selfishness, Philippians 2:3).

3. Find two verses, one dealing with peace and the other with patience, that will help you cultivate this fruit. Share the verses with your group.

4. In what way do you struggle to display the fruit of gentleness, goodness, and faithfulness? Yield these areas to the Lord in prayer.

5. Meekness and temperance are not popular in today's culture. Find Bible verses that share the truth about these characteristics. Talk about them with your group.

6. How did the Lord challenge you through this study? Give specific examples.

86558697R00126

Made in the USA
Columbia, SC
03 January 2018